DUMPED O,
BOND MARKET SPITS CRISES!

C. Fiifi Odoom

University Press of America,® Inc.
Lanham · Boulder · New York · Toronto · Plymouth, UK

Library of Congress Control Number: 2011930161
ISBN: 978-0-7618-5617-7 (paperback : alk. paper)
eISBN: 978-0-7618-5618-4

Table of Contents

Table of Contents

List of Figures

List of Tables

Preface

There has always been a chapter in the book on capitalist forms that feature key characters as exemplars of sorts. The memorable ones showcased in the recent (early 2008) one were not noted for virtues when the epilogue was read but rather their infamy. This has been a familiar story written over and over every decade or so, on the potency of phantom money - credit, in particular - the core of most capitalist forms. In bubble economies like ours dominated by oligopolistic production structures, credit takes life to stratospheric levels. Literally, the sky is the limit in this world driven by the bond market. Even marginal borrowers get to access credit by just paying an entrance fee of above-average interest rates consistent with their 'junk' status for, as long as good times rolls on, each side of the transaction benefits. Borrower access what they could not afford; lenders get above normal 'price' (interest rate) for their loans; jobs could be created in the process; and governments get tax windfall. As for those who rely on capital income like the Madoffs, they need to churn up even higher returns too to keep up with asset price bubbles around them and to support their lifestyle. This is where Bernie Madoff made himself useful.

Madoff is a character that comes around once in a decade, long enough for capitalisms to shed a layer of skin or two to pave way for the other(s). The decade before Madoff, the exotic genious was the now born-again Michael Milken, the junk bond impresario who ended up in prison for securities market fraud. But minimizing our own role in propping up such systems merely elevates these crooks into geniuses. The truth is that credit indeed is more than a facilitator of transactions. It is therapy, and, again, the bond market is always available to accommodate us to a point now where it has become a genetic marker in our acquisition quests and socially, we are paying a price for this credit culture.

Credit makes the relative poor spend more than they would have without such phantom cash. As for the well off, they gain disproportionately via leveraging and other forms of bets. That is what 'derivatives' are all about, bets that attracts the relatively wealthy. But the social cost that emerge in the most virulent forms whenever such credit bubble burst spreads the pain rather disproportionately rather disproportionately toward the relative poor rather than away from them. That is, if the benefits and costs were to be confined to private spaces during such crises times, criticism of such capitalist form would be mute but this is not usually the case.

Weakened balance sheet (deflated assets relative to liabilities) easily wipes off the relative poor's worth, and that of marginal (new) entrants considered 'Ponzi financiers'. The well established, on the otherhand, get to keep a chunk of spoils even after bankruptcy. 'Last to be hired, first to be fired', so the street lingo goes. Maxed out after such asset deflation, we become even more reliant on the bond market as Holy Grail to sustain even a downsized lifestyle. Thus, whether in prosperity or in recession, the art is to find ways to respond to such nagging internal (fiscal) and even external (current account) imbalances. Expenditure constriction - employee layoffs and cuts in public works projects – becomes the favourite method to mediate the transition from one form to the other. This is the debt culture at work, our new normal, and the bond market, as always, will provide the formal enabling arrangements for all that.

What size a (straight) bond market am I referring to? A scan through Bank of Settlement data has it at US$80 trillion by the end of the year 2009, way more than the estimated yearly world income (GDP) of around $50 trillion. The United States alone, though only one of the 192 countries on earth and with 25% of world annual income ends up dumping (borrowing) an estimated 43% of the value of this bond market. In otherwords it borrows close to double its income. The EU zone's numbers are not significantly different from the U.S. Put together, we have a huge debt load at hand. This is just a starter to this giant liquidity window that over-spenders get their fix from. The real meat of these funds is bets on this $80 trillion.

Even after significant asset deflation from the 2008 crisis, these bets (derivatives) on this 'underlying' $80 trillion and related real estate segment come up to $1.048 quadrillion, if we are to believe M12G Group[1] and Bank for International Settlement data, an amount 20 times the world GDP. An uninformative calculation put this at $140,000 per person on earth.

Of this gigantic derivatives market, over-the-counter (off the books) derivatives takes up almost 60% meaning that of this and exchange-traded (listed) credit derivatives 40%, a lion's share of the two values being bets on interest rate ($440 trillion), credit default, and foreign exchange close behind. A breakdown of principal actors are as follows.

1.   Consumers have (a) $4.5 outstanding credit card (b) $41 trillion residential property and an (c) estimated $1.2 trillion sub-prime-connected loans, and $10-trillion U.S. home mortgage market

2.   For businesses the close to (a) $4-trillion commodities market consisting of commodities derivatives and other commodities claims (b) the almost $36 trillion credit default swaps (c) the $21 trillion corporate bonds

market and d) $22 trillion commercial debt

3.   The $50 trillion foreign exchange derivatives market

Why such an unimaginable amounts?

Given the range of risks among borrowers and lenders, insurance is needed for protection against uncertainty. Second, market participants – be they lenders or borrowers - despite theoretical assurances, just do not trust the companies financial worth numbers out there, neither do they trust public ratings numbers that ratings agencies publish. A third group comprises of speculators. They place layers of bets on existing financial papers and/or commodities, adding another layer to the amplified value. The last group is cautious participants seeking to protect themselves against loses, hedgers, we call them. Put together, such phantom money keep such unproductive activities up, some seeking to protect existing assets, others just speculating on the assets several times over. In otherwords:

- Those with assets/receivables negotiate insurance/derivatives to protect the worth of their wares, creating duplication in the worth of the same assets and of GDP
- Some purchasers of such 'insurance' seek to protect their assets from falling in value, and their liabilities from increasing in value
- customers and financial institutions place insurance/derivative clauses in bonds in order to be able to alter the character of straight bonds so as to conceal some scams, or artificially raise commissions/premiums from such insurance
- Speculators buy derivatives to bet on a positions with expectation of gains, or to preserve gains
- For financial institutions, it is a way to protect themselves against borrowers, many of whom they hardly know but are referenced by credit agencies, themselves not that credible.

Collectively, we call a segment of this vast network of arrangements over over-the-counter market. Over-the-counter because, literally, it is over-our-heads in terms of quantity, quality, clarity, and specificity that we are used to in tightly regulated markets. Put together, with all these clauses and layers of supposed protections, it is understandable that even those who think they are experts in this market hardly understand them until the unexpected.

Even those who understand the contracts (and there are just a few of them) many a time forget that the bad 'event(s)' that premium are supposed to buy off tends to be inadequate to make up for effect of major accidents, let alone catastrophic ones. And as in all of such bets, someone (lender) stands to lose premiums whether the bad event happens or not. Otherwise the seller of the contract is happy, which usually is the case, a precipitator for the writing of even more risky contracts just for the premiums and fees. If fortune changes and goes the other way, then these gamblers (writers of the contracts) have to pay up. The sheer number of such losers lead to a flood of loses that could reverberate, drawing in even those with no part of the transaction other than the fact that they are geographically connected to buyers and sellers of the contracts. That is what happened to many banks in Europe and the United States in 2007, the runoff to the financial meltdown that is still playing itself out.

Note

1. Mi2.com (2010) article titled "Derivatives Quadrillion Play: How Far Away are We from a Second Financial Crisis" Mar 23, 2010.

Introduction:
The Virtues

The Reach, and the mainstreaming of the Bond Market

An executive from the Gillette division of Procter & Gamble revealed, in a June 2008 interview with BBC, that their first 'sensitive skin' product introduced fifty years ago was for a niche market – for the select few identifying with 'sensitive skin'. It was intended for it to stay that way, as a niche product. Over time though, he argued, his product did not change but people did. Most of us now believe we have sensitive skins. All of a sudden, a product that had not changed was thrown into a mass market where almost everyone now find *essential*. The bond market is in such a unique position as well.

No longer is it an exclusive golf course for governments and mega corporations. The masses have been emboldened to play there too, a massive market for all with the thirst for deals, for virtually anything – car, consumer goods, mortgages, pay shortfalls (payday loans), student expenses, bridges, employee payroll etc – thanks to the little bond*lets* made available by *securitization,* innovation that permit even illiquid assets such as houses and contracts to be turned into liquid cash by a click of a mouse. This is why this (straight bond) market has ballooned to an estimated $1-trillion-a-day market. There is a third dimension to this mainstreaming of the bond market.

Matured Economies struggles

Growth theorists will say that 'matured' economies have had their turn at growth. What goes up must come down to get to *steady state*, a natural condition where natural growth is just enough to compensate for wear and tear. But then came the bond market, in a big way, as a turbo engine of sorts. The chart below points to this with the negative entries as net asset positions (borrowings).

Table 1.1: Net Foreign Asset Positions of OECD Countries (Percent of GDP)

	1990	2000	2003(1)	2003(2)
Australia	-47.4	-65.2	-59.1	-74
Austria				-22
Belgium				34
Canada	-38.0	-30.6	-20.6	-21
Denmark		-21.5	-13.0	-20
Finland	-29.2	-58.2	-35.9	-28
France				4
Germany				8
Greece				-60
Iceland	-48.2	-55.5	-66.0	-82
Italy				-10
Japan				37
Netherlands				-15
New Zealand	-88.7	-120.8	-131.0	-90
Norway				45
Portugal				-64
Spain				-45
Sweden	-26.6	-36.7	-26.5	0
Switzerland				145
United Kingdom				-6
United States				
Direct investment at current cost	-4.2	-14.1	-19.6	-19.6
Direct investment at market prices	-2.8	-16.1	-21.6	-21.6

Source: OECD

Growth, undoubtedly, has been a key motivator for policymakers push into bonds. As will be argued shortly, indiscipline also plays a large part. But for other market participants, generous commissions and fees blinds them to downplay significant downside seen largely as theoretical probabilities but could become all too real. This is the 'moral hazards' we have come to know so much of from insurance practitioners to refer to high-flying 'drifters' in the credit market who survive in good time but have enough question marks to be of concern in normal times. In fact the better the times, the more reckless these financial institutions get on such generous debt issues. Under this environment, all it takes is just a minor shock for the Ponzi traps to go off, for borrowers to default on their loans and for lenders to lose out on expected profits. Thus, 'profit' turn into massive loses, and the dominos filter through the entire system – real and financial sectors. Fears of collapse of these lending institutions deemed 'too big to fail' elicit intense lobbying of taxpayers to foot the bill. Blackmailed to believe that unless they pay up the financial system will collapse, taxpayers relent.

At a more deeper level of engagement, the oddity of the bond market is that it is one of the few (markets) out there that it:

- provides an intergenerational platform for discourse over all aspects of social imperatives needing a secure finance outlet. We have a Trust Fund arrangement that relies on the bond market as a key investment vehicle to tie generations together via a pay-as-you-go formula that has the young pay for the old. The more popular one of late is the sister program under the label 401K. Individuals, here, self-save, usually matched by employers or the state, or exempted from some taxes. Under both programs, bonds are seen as safe haven to tuck away most of such funds. All kinds of institutions - institutional investors – emerged since the post-wars to fill the knowledge gap of how to spread risks for decent return.

- Sure, this bond market cannot explain how Tiger Woods economic value was sliced in half overnight upon news of personal indiscretion, or how Elliot Spitzer fell from grace from New York governor's chair for fooling around with a call girl. But it can explain, convincingly, why Iceland's value was sliced by over 80%, and still taking a toll on the U.S., U.K., and other club members.

- Even though also cannot explain adequately how value can be pulled from under the rubble at Port-au-Prince after the January 2010 earthquake, we have made a case that similar social projects are made easier with the bond market.

- More importantly for my purpose, it can shed light on how economic agents, working behind the facade of the market's purity, in search for the more illusive value, could be left vulnerable, seemingly unaware that the safety of bonds, as per financial theory, is incompatible with the exotics that new innovations (securitizations) brings. Either way, one thing is certain. The bond market started of as a one-stop place for all kinds of good social projects. It is where:

a. Governments secure a bulk of its funds of late; get a bulk of its hard currency by sitting at home and issuing its sovereign (foreign currency denominated) bonds

b. for consumers, this market is a hedge against all kinds of economic adversity: more than a space for financial instruments to fly through. It is a safe haven for their savings and/or investments

c. Social good proponents see a coalescence of thoughts on a neutral ground to finance post-War reconstruction dreams

d. For *labor value* theorists, the bond market symbolizes how value could be created far beyond the real-side of the economy posited by classical economists: Scottish Adam Smith, British David Ricardo, and German Karl Marx. They traced value to labor, focusing on intrinsic-valued items like gold, diamond whose values are derived from mainly labor put in them. From the other end is Post-Keynesian Economists and other *market-exchange* value-creating enthusiasts who see the bond market as emblematic of the art of creating money and value from thin air to add to such old-fashioned value created by labor. To them, money created in this market are means as much as they are ends (value) in themselves.

e. In 1989, some Development economists joined in the bond fray by touting the Brady Bond as not only commodities of sorts but also a development agents key to converting Latin America's indebtedness into tradable IOUs

f. Financing wars became hip. Henry Morgenthau, the then Finance Minister (Secretary of the Treasury), in addition to adding state muscles to such assurances, was himself given assurances of the bond market as a reliable source of funds to finance the major wars and for reconstruction effort. For the older generation on the verge of retiring, an expansive government was an extension of a vibrant and emerging welfare state that increasingly had Social Security as a cocktail and a defacto extended family in regions outside the Mediterranean. For the ethically edgy, there was a little something for them too. Such savings was seen not only as fiscally prudent and from investment perspective wise but also benevolent. Thus, the 1935 year a watershed of such finance The state got to receive the much-needed liquidity that otherwise would remained idle. This was the birth of the U.S. Savings Bond. Canada followed suit with a 'victory bond' to celebrate the 1939-1945 war that eventually came to be known as Canada Savings Bond.

g. But for those who think the aforementioned benefits of this market are too good to be true, perhaps they are, considering where we have mixed up our social and private value missions. We have even managed to rely on this market to pay compensation for our unemployed, finance job training projects, provide assistance for our smaller governments, lead anti-poverty fights, renewable energy, emergency projects, and countless social projects. Thus, this extension of our traditional money-churning machines has managed to tie us, celestially, to social and economic values of all kinds, values that, unfortunately, could take other countries down as well sectors and across spaces.

Items (a)-(h) will be sketched in the same reverend light that the bond market has historically been cast but (g) will receive the most attention here. To do this we have to go beyond the traditional narrations of the objects (IOUs) as liquid, value stability, measurable returns. We are culturally immersing ourselves in it without even knowing it. It all began in earnest when anxious societies were desperately seeking all kinds of values at different levels of polities after the Great Depression distorted and realigned worth, giving room for all kinds of worth creation. Enter the bond market.

Dumping dysfunction

The bond market has always been a fertile ground for the recycling of savings. But now, it has also become a dumping ground for societal excesses. Shopperholics need not worry here. Their condition can be controlled with a visit to the bond market with a click of a mouse. Have a discipline problem at the budgetary front? Call on the bond market. Need insurance for the intractable? Call on the bond market. Nervous about all the shades of characters in this market? Buy an 'insurance' from its west wing – derivative market – to protect self from the unforeseen. As stated earlier, this derivatives market, from what we can tell from the BIS data, is a $600 trillion one, almost 12 times the world's GDP of $55 trillion. Why such an unimaginable size of an insurance market?

First, the few rich countries that generate most of this $55 trillion get to bet on their incomes several times over because their thirst for credit dictates such 'insurance' given the range of risks among borrowers and lenders alike. Simply put, we buy insurance to cover uncertainty. This is where the derivative market takes its spiritual strength. Second, market participants – be they lenders or borrowers - despite theoretical assurances, just do not trust the companies financial worth numbers out there, neither do they trust public ratings numbers that ratings agencies publish. A third group comprises of speculators. They place layers of bets on existing financial papers and/or commodities, adding another layer to the amplified value. The last group is cautious participants seeking to protect themselves against loses, hedgers, we call them. Put together, all such phantom money keeps such unproductive activities up around phantom money, some seeking to protect existing assets, others just speculating on the assets several times over. In otherwords:

- Those with assets/receivables negotiate insurance/derivatives to protect the worth of their wares, creating duplication in the worth of the same assets and of GDP
- Some purchasers of such 'insurance' seek to protect their assets from falling in value, and their liabilities from increasing in value
- customers and financial institutions place insurance/derivative clauses in bonds in order to be able to alter the character of straight bonds so as to conceal some scams, or artificially raise commissions/premiums from such insurance
- Speculators buy derivatives to bet on a positions with expectation of gains, or to preserve gains
- For financial institutions, it is a way to protect themselves against borrowers, many of whom they hardly know but are referenced by credit agencies, themselves not that credible.

Collectively, we call a chunk of this vast network of arrangements *over over-the-counter* market. Over-the-counter because, literally, it is over-our-heads in terms of quantity, quality, clarity, and specificity that we are used to in tightly regulated markets. Put together, with all these clauses and layers of supposed protections, no wonder we hardly understand the contracts until the unexpected hit.

Even those who work in this market many a time forget that the bad 'event(s)' that premium are supposed to buy off tend to be inadequate to make up for effect of major accidents.

As in all of such bets, someone (lender) stands to lose premiums whether the bad event happens or not. If it does not happen, the seller of the contract is happy but if it does, bad news. If it is a large event, then 'mass killing', the state was there to bail them out fearing that the bill will be large enough to run them out of business so it had to step in.

Ideally, if it were flood insurance, so long as no flood shows up, insurance companies are very happy to keep your premiums. Once flood hit, however, they get swamped. All of a sudden contracts come due from all over, maybe contracts that the companies should not have written in such numbers but because good times have rolled on for so long a time, the premiums were, literally, freebies, so they kept writing, ignoring the risk of flood. Ultimately, they get swamped and when the event hits paying up is a problem. That is what happened to many banks in Europe and the United States in 2007, the runoff to the financial meltdown that is still playing itself out. But, as always, you, as the taxpayer, whether you were a party to those transactions or not, have to pay up to bail them out.

Section 1
The Virtues

Chapter 1
Commoners Join In: Bonds for Shopping, Bonds as Paychecks

Our changing world now has a bond market that is no longer for the elite fraternities of governments and big businesses. Anyone can access it for infinite needs — to take payday or other loans, or to accommodate requisitions from a Microsoft, a Hewlett Packard, or a central government. This section elaborates on the reach of this gigantic moneymaking mall that happens to represent only one side of the conversation (the demand side). Subsequent sections build on this demand side with supply-side constrictions.

At the supply side is a lesson in financial "old-fashionedism," which the beloved Warren Buffet reinforced when the economy tanked in 2008. While warning of the increasing influence of kleptocrats at the helms of both corporate and political bureaucracies — Schumpeterian in spirit — he touted the Swedish model of corporate finance — again, an old-fashioned idea (dual share arrangement) as a desirable and enduring arrangement. Warren did it again by shelling out $26 billion on November 3, 2009 to buy out Burlington Northern Santa Fe Corporation, a relic and a line of business (railways) that launched the (Charles) Dow Jones index in the eighteenth century. He "saved" America using his own old-fashioned methods, with a plain vanilla strategy of lending in simple terms (preferred stocks) at a time when many sat on the sidelines. This man exuded a confidence in the financial system, a posture that encouraged others to join in. Reeling from his losses in derivatives during his first go at it — instruments that he admits he knows little about, while remaining of the view that they are of limited benefit — he pulled preferred stocks out of his old-fashioned toolbox for a reason. This stock/bond hybrid that is listed on stock exchanges pays dividends of sorts, and has inscription negotiated with a simple trigger made to kick into either a stock or a bond once conditions become (un)favorable. Such an instrument comes in handy when no one is lending. To the borrower, preferred stocks make sense because they protect investors such as Warren with an insurance of sorts, meant to keep them from losing their shirts in case the company tanks, but with a chance to win big in times of prosperity. This insurance comes in the form of a predetermined bargain price. In case of a market rally, Warren would make a killing, and boy, he has cleaned up since the crisis, because the companies he lent to rallied nicely. All he needs to do is buy their shares at bargain-basement prices, to be resold at higher prices. Thus, this book reinforces what we have been hearing from Congress lately: Rather than high tech, low tech in savings and in plain vanilla corporate relationships could be the key to preventing swings in values — the essence of financial crisis.

Introduction

In a May 8th 2009 interview with the British Broadcasting Company (BBC) on the new Gillette product Gillette Fusion, a professor and a Gillette executive stated that his company's first "sensitive skin" product, introduced fifty years ago, was for a niche market — the select few who identified with "sensitive skin." It was intended to stay that way, as a niche product. Over time, he argued, his product did not change but people did. Most of us now believe we have sensitive skin. All of a sudden, a product that had not changed was thrown into a mass market where almost everyone now finds it essential. The bond market is in such a unique position as well. No longer is it an exclusive golf course for governments and mega-corporations. The masses have been emboldened to play there, too — all shades of people with a thirst for deals to finance even necessities, especially their mix of vainglories — cars, consumer goods, mortgages, pay shortfalls (payday loans), student expenses, dental work, employee payrolls, etc. This is thanks to the little bondlets made available by securitization, an innovation that permits receivables and even illiquid assets to be turned into liquid cash by the click of a mouse. Let us pull the real side into this financial story to make it complete for us, and to let us see how the mainstreaming of bonds could very well undermine financial stability.

Real-Side, Anyone?

A July 2, 2010 op-ed piece in *The New York Times* entitled "Are Profits Hurting Capitalism?" was all too real for me to pass up, for the simple reason that it fits tightly into the context sketched here. On the face of it, one would wonder how profit could hurt capitalism when capitalism rests on profits. But upon closer examination, it makes sense. Our credit card culture supports a new debt threshold that can accommodate corporations without "profits." After all, governments, like consumers, routinely make charges on their (bond market) credit cards when they overspend (when they run deficits). Of these three economic agents — consumers, governments, and corporations — only corporations made money/profits in the last two decades, but they are not spending. Surprise? Not quite! We have known this for a while, that piling up such savings makes quarterly earnings look pretty, what Wall Street likes to see. Such hoards, we know, help pay off high-priced executives, pay dividends to shareholders, and aid in speculation — typically in buying up the competition through mergers and acquisitions. We would be tempted to think that the future benefits of such savings, from the corporate point of view, do not outweigh the present one of dividend payouts. Thus, Smith and Parenteau (2010) suggest, in the *New York Times* article, that governments should realign incentives for these corporations to join in on the spending culture, too. Otherwise, they argued, we will sink back into recession, especially if governments rid themselves of their credit cards, even if just temporarily. Overspending clearly pays. One specific prescription Smith and Parenteau suggested was a tax on the turnover of such corporate finance.

The objective is to raise the cost of speculation, and to impose a tax on retained earnings, to keep corporations from hoarding such cash. Certainly, they admit that balancing their books will cool demand for goods and services, and lead to layoffs. Cooling prices translates into higher debt load, because $100 owed today could be worth, say, $105 in a year's time. That means consumers who happen to be laid off end up being stuck with a higher debt load.

As for governments, raising taxes could balance their books, but ends up reducing taxpayer's paychecks, and so do expenditure cuts. That could be even more devastating, because it leads directly to job cuts. Continued overspending does just that: it props up jobs and demand. So, we are stuck with an old habit that all of us — consumers, corporations, and governments — cannot even begin to come to grips with. So, back to my thesis.

What does Smith and Parenteau's (2010) "profit for dividend payout" thesis have to do with the bond market? What has the new Japanese Prime Minister's June 11, 2010 maiden speech to the Japanese parliament got to do with the bond market? What have demonstrations against government cutbacks to social services and the wages of government employees in Athens, Lisbon, London, Madrid, Los Angeles, Reykjavik, and Dublin got to do with the bond market? On March 15, 2010, 93% of Icelandic voters said "no" to a $5 billion-plus-debt load payable to British and Dutch lenders. What has that got to do with the bond market? Jon Gnarr, an Icelandic comedian, had founded the Best Party five months before this "no" vote. His election platform consisted of building Disneyland at the airport for kids, displaying polar bears at the zoo, giving out free towels at public pools, and making Parliament drug free. On such a ridiculous platform, he got elected Mayor of Reykjavik. What has Gnarr's election got to do with the bond market? What has your car or payday loan got to do with the bond market? I will establish this in the very next chapter — but first, here is an intriguing variant on this story that now takes me to the spending culture in Illinois.

Blago in Illinois

Remember Blago? His real name is Rod Blagojevich, and he was the fortieth Governor of the state of Illinois (2003–2009) around the time Illinois favorite son Barack Obama was running for President of the United States. Blago made national and international headlines with his high-profile arrest for trying to sell Barack Obama's vacant Senate seat. Even for Chicago "pay-to-play" politics,

Blago brought added excitement to a state that has been, throughout the twentieth century, a movie capital for gangsters and corrupt political culture. At a deeper level of corruption, however, Blago is just one of the boys — no better and no worse.

This is a state that has had two of its former governors thrown in jail, and another presently on trial for similar indiscretions. Blago just happened to be reckless enough to get caught red-handed in the middle of presidential politics. This is "Chicago Politics" with a twist. But there is another reality in the State House, which is that Blago just played to the crowd, legally, and was cheered on the same as his predecessors; Blago simply made it into a work of art. In Powell's (2010) [1.] words, Blago shed the Democratic "tax-and-spend" image for a slick "spend and borrow" label. This earned Illinois membership in a not-so-exclusive club that has California and New York as members. A postscript has all the three states teetering on the edge of bankruptcy, with all the hallmarks of indiscipline, now in hindsight unexpected of a state (Illinois) that habitually took pension holidays to avoid paying into pension funds, (50% estimated unfunded status), and with a legislature, bi-partisan in spirit on this scheme, that routinely ignored passing budgets or having the guts to raise taxes to close the giant holes in them. It was hip at the time.

The result is that the unfunded liability position for Illinois pension funds alone stands at more than twice the entire state budget. It is desperation time. Law enforcement personnel and school personnel are being laid off. Other state and local government employees are also being put on notice. So, when you hear of the doubling of the unemployment rate from less than 5% in 2006 to almost 12% four years later, and housing starts screeching to a halt, what should come to mind is the enabling bond market that permits us to ride the highs only to trip and come back down to earth occasionally — once every decade, as the pattern goes. Whether this has something to do with the bond market or not — and I argue that it does — it happens that the relatively poor get to keep a chunk of the spoils, not so with the relatively rich. What has the bond market got to do with the recent financial crisis? Implications of these two questions on economic theory are discussed throughout this book. To start the discussion, a few factoids on our dissavings culture are in order.

The Struggles of Mature Countries

Growth theory follows natural law, that we cannot grow forever and that what goes up must come down, somehow. The same applies to countries. Growth numbers have slowed to a crawl for the poorer ones, who must "catch up" and converge at their respective steady states. It is analogous to group of short people having to grow and converge, and taller ones having to do the same. So these groups of countries end up converging on particular consumption/savings paths shaped by technological conditioning. But the bond market (Table 1 below) came to the rescue in the way it provided fiscal stimulus internally through fiscal deficits, even paving the way for countries to veer into negative foreign asset positions. Table 1.1 below shows how virtually all these OECD countries went into deficit positions way before the crisis hit.

Table 1.1: Net Foreign Asset Positions of OECD Countries (Percent of GDP)

	1990	2000	2003(1)	2003(2)
Australia	-47.4	-65.2	-59.1	-74
Austria				-22
Belgium				34
Canada	-38.0	-30.6	-20.6	-21
Denmark		-21.5	-13.0	-20
Finland	-29.2	-58.2	-35.9	-28
France				4
Germany				8
Greece				-60
Iceland	-48.2	-55.5	-66.0	-82
Italy				-10
Japan				37
Netherlands				-15
New Zealand	-88.7	-120.8	-131.0	-90
Norway				45
Portugal				-64
Spain				-45
Sweden	-26.6	-36.7	-26.5	0
Switzerland				145
United Kingdom				-6
United States				
Direct investment at current cost	-4.2	-14.1	-19.6	-19.6
Direct investment at market prices	-2.8	-16.1	-21.6	-21.6

Source: OECD

Note

1. Michael Powell, "Illinois Stops Paying Its Bills, But Can't Stop Digging Hole." New York Times, 3 July 2010.

References

Kregel, J. Observations on the Problem of "Too Big to Fail/Save/Resolve." Policy Note 2009/11, Levy Economics Institute paper, December 2010.

Kregel, J. No Going Back: Why We Cannot Restore Glass–Steagal's Segregation of Banking and Finance. Levy Economics Institute paper No. 107A, 2010.

Minsky, H. *Stabilizing an Unstable Economy*. New York: McGraw-Hill, 1986.

Chapter 2
After Greek Food, the Diet

Introduction

Debt (or "credit," as we like to call it) has become a right of passage for individuals and businesses. Governments, too, are expected to use it "for the public good" when bad times arrive. As for the average consumer, "good credit" (debt) is a *must have* for concessionary credit. The same goes for businesses. Debt even helps pump up their value via acquisition of the competition. This gives the impression that something new is going on besides the same ole stuff. C'mon, this is the essence of the endless new products/editions that come to the market by the minute. For corporations, it is key to speculating on the direction of their (stock) prices.

Borrowing Even in Good Times

In good times, we tend to have the means to save, but with interest rates artificially low — thanks to easy-money monetary policy and securitization — the draw is more spending. Even developing countries are in on this, but for them it is a pro-business appeal as key developmental tool. Looking at fig. 1, we have both consumers and businesses responding rationally with extravagantly high business debt as per economic theory to such a low "price" of money. Debt here is too cheap for shoppers to pass up. Again, as per economic theory, the more economically well off a country is, chances are the better the access to even more such credit. In automobile parlance, credit becomes the horsepower that drives the internal combustion (credit) economic engine. With this horsepower, it does not really matter whether a country is internationally "competitive" or not. In good economic times it survives anyway, and in bad times, thanks to this bond market and the fuel it supplies to the engine, countries have another window. This is the situation in which the Club Med (Italy, Spain, Portugal, and Greece) found itself in the decade prior to the 2008 financial meltdown.

High-growth environments created expectations that even better times lay ahead, an environment that made credit acquisition a rational choice of payment arrangement. A good chunk of these impulse borrowers were motivated to dig even deeper into the equity (savings) in their homes, and into even more debt. Over-indulgence is the key here: consumers acting on emotions and the corporate sector touting growth without necessarily growing. As for the hard numbers, Figure 2.1 tells of household and financial debt being functions of economic growth and development. The richer the country, the more consumer spending there is as a percentage of total debt. In the relatively poor BRIC countries (Brazil, Russia, India, and China), however, consumer spending is a function of GDP per person, so being relatively poor reduces spending ability. Yet in bad times the pendulum seems to swing the other way, with poorer countries more resilient.

Figure 2.1: Debt as a Percent of GDP, 2008

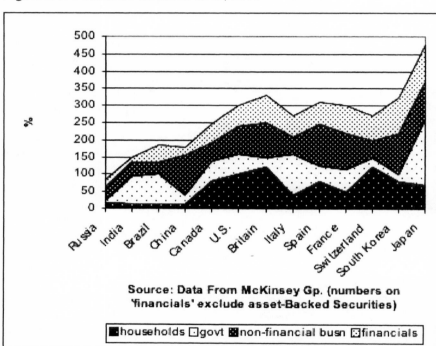

The Bond Market as We Know It

For a moment, let us go beyond the benign, exotic, and even glamorous slant on textbook portrayals of bonds and the large market that they trade in. This familiar story has bonds as special IOU certificates issued by special companies, the best being governments. These borrowers even get to borrow from special agents like banks who in turn are supposed to vet potential lenders. A number of these "loans" are actually put together by yet another unique group of intermediaries called underwriters — agents in business who match such special borrowers to lenders, the most special of these being institutional lenders.

For governments, there are even special agents called brokers, skilled loyalists who do the legwork for four types of quality IOUs that the Treasury or Finance Department commandeers on behalf of the federal government. You might have heard of them as the four Ts — T-bills, T-notes, T-bonds, and T-IPS (Treasury, Inflation Protected Securities). In the year 2008 — just when the turmoil was simmering — in the United States, $6.7 trillion worth of market value could be traced to these four Ts, or well over half of U.S. GDP — and that is just a start. The numbers for 2010 are still rolling in.

These special salespeople (brokers) start their sales by announcing the dates of auction, which depend upon the maturity date of the IOUs). An interested buyer merely submits an offer of purchase for the IOUs, at a discount of, for example, 2% or 3% "off." If accepted, the IOUs are sold and delivered by the brokers, who demand that checks be written, or that "credit cards" to be used to pay. More importantly, the accepted discounts that lenders are offered end up being the "price" for lending, the preeminent and the benchmark price that we refer to as "risk-free" rates. This metric spins off other interest rates available to less credible (junk) companies, who have little choice but to "discount" their issues significantly from the face value, for being riskier than Treasury Department bonds. In other words, they have to pay more for not being household names.

Irrespective of the risk characteristics, three special companies are entrusted with the responsibility for assigning the spreads reflected in discount rates that lenders bid for. Treasuries' "risk-free" rates is distinguished from the not-so-prime bond rates out there. Here comes the problem — well, actually, five of them.

First, these special companies — the federal government included — are increasingly being exposed as mediocre, overextended, and "overpriced" as good credit, and on the verge of losing their AAA credit ratings. Second, what happens when so many such companies, moneymakers and money-losers alike, are all borrowing money from this new one-stop bond market, making it difficult to place them on the spread chart for appropriate interest rates to be charged? The third question is related to the first. What if lenders are distrustful of these same spreads and the derivative quality of such companies? They resort to self-help and issue insurance/derivatives, such as credit default swaps. At least on paper, they hedge against such uncertainty. Fourth, what if such derivatives generate so much money in "premiums" that they become a cash cow that regulators (central banks and other regulatory agencies) entrusted with oversight find it prudent to look the other way rather than rein them in and trade them in organized exchanges, downplaying potential dangers as if we were immune? Fifth, what if consumers and hedge funds join in this borrowing binge with credit cards hooked up to securitization — the art of turning a number of illiquid assets into instant cash to lend?

By the end of the year 2007, according to the latest figures available, outstanding U.S. government debt from the aforementioned deals stood at a third of the estimated world figure of about $83 trillion — a good 50% more than the estimated world GDP of $55 trillion. In other words, imagine owing 50% more than you make in income. This is not all. Year after year, since 2009, the U.S. government has been spending more than 60% of what the country makes (GDP) on this "bond market credit card." This leaves around 40% of GDP for all other things that governments traditionally spend money on.

I am not even counting the numerous IOUs that are not recorded, especially ones stemming from three key demand pressures on governments: the demand for social expenditures from the left, tax cuts from the right, as well as unforeseen incidentals that come with a mix of social projects: pressures from cyclical downturns, activism, wars (on terror and drugs, for example), foreign aid, and research projects. Then there are the relatively new consumer demands for fancy cars, houses, furniture, travel, and education, all of which are burdens put on credit cards issued on the bond market. These exist in addition to other business and hedge fund demands. In short, the bond market is a dumping ground for our wider enabling society.

More Moral Reasons to Go Into the Bond Market, and Into Debt

As stated earlier, developing countries' principal objective for borrowing is to enhance public space. This is what most of the BRIC countries' government spending reflects, supported by the 2001 Merrill Lynch Research Report pointing to the 75% of public debt issues in Korea, 81% in India, and 41% in China. In richer countries, with the notable exception of Japan, spurts in government spending mirror the way automatic stabilizers are supposed to work. That is, in bad times, governments are supposed to step up to their paternalistic role and provide a cushion for the 'needy'. This is the Keynesian counter-cyclical prescription ("stimulus") that we have heard so much of lately, one aspect of it being expenditure boosts to create jobs, and the other for companies and the relatively wealthy — who get to take a fatter take home pay from tax cuts. On top of these, one can pull in the benefit from monetary (lower interest rate) policy, which gives all agents the incentive to spend even more.

Among all these countries, Japan is the only one whose spending goes way beyond the call of spending duty. Its debt of close to 500% of its income/GDP did not come about by accident. It is a high-cultural tradition, boosted by productivity surges in the 1970s and 1980s that ended up neutralizing the high interest rates that hindered large internal borrowing there. In the subsequent climate, Japan became indebted to itself (i.e., internal debt), with its government (the borrower) paying interest to its own people. Continued high-productivity kept interest rates in check for the currency (the *yen*) to remain competitive as well. As a consequence, Japan could still maintain strong current account surplus. It still does. Not so with other countries.

The PIIGGS (Portugal, Ireland, Italy, Great Britain, Greece, Spain; see Figure 2.2) had a hard time keeping their competitive heads above water. Selling

less relative to what they bought to the rest of the world over time gradually
deteriorated their balance sheets. That was why they had to resort to borrowing
to finance their consumption. In so doing, the PIIGGS drove up the risk of their
debt position (note the rising CDS, credit default swaps) and spreads, reflecting
in such fears. More often than not, in such cases, yields increase, a clear sign of
higher risk associated with such excessive demand. But for borrowers steeped in
this credit tradition, a cut in credit is seen as a growth-buster. The same goes with
lenders: they lose the high-return business, especially from marginal borrowers.

Figure 2.2: OECD Standard of Living, Per Capita

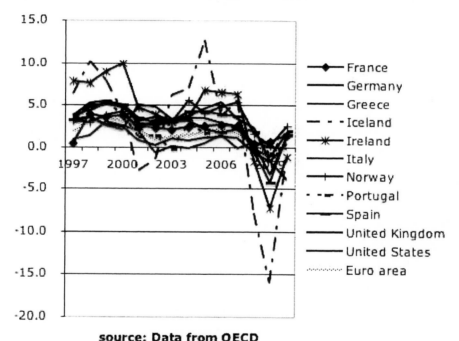

source: Data from OECD

Can Islam Convert Such Debtors?

Unlike Indiviglio, [2.] albeit just as provocatively, I am not quite suggesting
that we criminalize credit, although doing that would remove a lot of the
unpredictability in financial markets that we have today. Though the United States
and the PIIGGS would not be able to borrow that much on behalf of the world,
we could still buy homes, but with old-fashioned cash, or by way of lease. We
can also make other rental arrangements, but again, not with the easy bank loans
that we now get through the bond market. Such a cultural shift will dampen the
demand for houses, naturally, taking construction jobs on such houses with it
on loan contraction. So in this Islamic world, cash and carry will be the order of
the day; although, for businesses, Letters of Credit and other such debit schemes

will still be in play because receivables could be proven. The ultimate result? Unemployment will rise as air is forced out of the bubble economies, but we will get used to it.

In fact, this and other moral arguments, especially the condemnation of usury, advocate the Islamic belief that money is not worth anything in itself (i.e., it has no intrinsic value) and therefore should not be used to make money via all kinds of moneymaking schemes (especially those with excessive interest rates). But let us put the virtues of credit aside, and return to my thesis that the bond market is venting its dissatisfaction over the way the United States and the PIIGGS have dumped their fiscal indiscipline on it through bond issues.

Crisis as a Starting Point

The voting public now is now familiar with the terms "financial crisis," "economic downturn," and "recession," thanks to news peddlers who have made such phrases available 24 hours a day. An interesting caveat of nonconforming mortgages "structured" as collateral has preoccupied a group of economists who have made a living on such debt packages as the driving force behind crises formation. This narration reminds me of the proverbial house built near the shore of an ocean. All it takes is a single once-in-a-decade "flood" to quickly make fools of such beach dwellers. But do not feel sorry for them at that moment — a *Minskyian Moment,* or so these Post-Keynesian economists call it.

This "flood" brings in deflation of cash receipts of marginal (Ponzi) borrowers relative to cash commitments. Simply put, declining net worth from both parties in transactions leads to massive defaults and consequential crisis. But even post-Keynesians miss this key bond market (superstructure) and its potency.

Regional Responses to the Aftershock

In his maiden address to Parliament on June 18, 2010, the new Japanese Prime Minister Naoto Kan warned that for the first time, the Japanese domestic bond market seemed incapable of taking any more of the state indiscipline reflected in the avalanche of bonds thrown at the bonds market. In other words, despite Japan's traditionally high savings rate, the state had been all too comfortable being accommodated and in turn accommodating the internal market. But all signs leads to this market maxing out. Perhaps this is the scariest part of Japanese public finance: reality that they will have to rely on foreigners to finance its indiscipline.

In other words, the supply of bonds is outstripping internal capacity to absorb them. As people age and change from savers to consumers of their own savings (with governments clawing back part of retirement income through taxation), a younger generation used to consuming more than they save complicates such savings efforts. Tag on the fact that this society has not warmed up to immigration, and one arrives at a society starved for new taxpayers at a time of declining birth rates. A realistic scenario for the state will likely be that its axe falls on spending. This is the demand side of the bond equation confronting a supply-side that had been propped up by Ricardian Equivalent belief that internal interest rates reward awaits them as a nationalistic duty. Clearly, this congregation could be losing followers to that of the PIIGGS, a people who have not quite accepted their destiny but hopes good times comes back soon to postpone whatever doomsday scenario they have been reminded so much of. In the meantime there are marginal changes to such old habits.

The Club Med — especially Spain — are talking seriously about a return to the 40-hour week, and lower wages for most public sector workers — ideas that are no longer received as crazy American and Asian practices. Yet on May 4, 2010, the establishment would not accept this lying down. A massive, and eventually violent, public demonstration in Athens, Greece, ended up with three bank employees dead. The bank, perceived as the symbol of capitalism that had failed the country, was set ablaze. Clearly, the demonstrators felt that their way of life would be disrupted, and from the trend in deficit culture shown in the chart above (Figure 2.4) and of public deficit growth in virtually all Western countries, it is of little surprise that the violence has spread to the rest of Euroland.

Notes

1. For a complete narration of the auction process, please visit http://www.treasurydirect.gov/instit/auctfund/work/auctime/auctime.htm
2. Daniel Indiviglio, "Criminalize Credit," *Atlantic Monthly,* 22 June 2010

Section 2
Mediating the Two Savings

Chapter 3
Public Dis(Savings)

Macroeconomics textbooks are big on the so-called twin deficits as desirable genetic markers. It is becoming clear, however, that even within similar species, different markers merely tell different stories of proclivities, not much more. Likewise, it is possible for countries to have one marker overseas — healthy foreign savings (in other words, a current account surplus), but another (dissavings/ budgetary deficit) at home. That is why it is the mix of private and foreign savings that counts, not necessarily the absolute amount of either. Once we sort out what actually binds the two together, then one can, hopefully, understand why it is common knowledge that the United States has a savings problem, what could very well be the Achilles Heel of the recovery efforts.

Introduction

This chapter is about aggregate savings/consumption habits. It goes like this. It is possible for a country to "save" and accumulate surplus by selling more to the outside world than it buys, and accumulate hard currency (savings) in the process. "Surplus" on the current account is another name for this, Japan being the exemplar and China a latecomer. But the two disciplinary realms could cross paths. In the past few decades, Japan accumulated fiscal deficits within its borders, recycled its private savings to make up for it, but then produced and sold more to foreign countries than it bought. This is Japanese and German engineering at its best — defy gravity up to a point. Now, the elements in this combo (fiscal position and private savings) are showing signs of strain. One has to be strengthened in order for the other to cooperate but so far it is the current account (surplus) that is the bright spot. We have yet to see it either re-orient domestic capacity for revenues to show an uptick or for expenditure to be contained. The worst-case scenario is to let this deficit define interest rates to become another source of fiscal strain.

In the United States, such rates are set by the Fed (central bank) and are influenced by quasi-money (government) agencies with the responsibility to make loans available to different risk groups. In effect just two of these institutions

- Fannie Mae and Freddie Mac - managed to mainstream this debt culture. A postscript: When they were seized after the 2008 meltdown, a regulator ordered these two juggernaut home mortgage agencies to voluntarily delist because they had little value as private companies. These two behemoths have fallen from almost $70 billion in value to almost nothing now. But do not cry for Fannie or Freddie. The U.S. government is bankrolling them.

The Public Savings Part

The public (nations) saves if it sells more than it buys to and from the rest of the world. It will be dissaving if it buys more than it sells.

Public savings

We get net positive savings if there is a positive (surplus) sum of:

1. receipts (tax revenues)
2. what
   - private producers sell to the government to be sold overseas, and
   - what the government by itself sells overseas and
   - to its people, and finally
3. Private savings
   - net of what "producers" sell.

If sum positive, it is savings and if negative, dissavings.

Figure 3.1: How a Country Saves

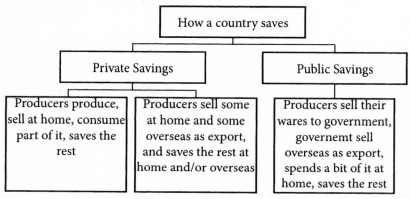

Relationship Between Public Dis(Savings) and Budgetary Deficit/Surplus

Budget deficit is the shortfall in what the government gets from its revenue sources (taxes and production) relative to what it spends. By September 2008, the number for the U.S. deficit was $6 trillion and projected to top 13% of GDP by the end of 2010, a reversal of the 2.5% surplus in 2000. Comparable numbers for other OECD countries rage from 16% deficit for U.K., up from the 7% surplus it had in 2000; 8% deficit for France, up from 1.8% deficit a decade earlier; Japan remarkably stable at about 8% deficit over the two decades; Canada a 5.1% deficit from a 3% surplus a decade earlier; and Euro area in general 7% deficit from an almost zero deficit in 2000.

We are not even counting the IOUs issued to borrow for the Social Security Trust Fund (in the case of the U.S., and similar related institution elsewhere) and the Federal Reserve, all outside budgetary calculation. Tag on the more than $1.3 trillion in stimulus funds, a figure that is still growing by the month, and we approach 70% of GDP for the U.S. by 2010. That is not all. "Contingent liabilities" are even more problematic, having been estimated at more than $8 trillion. These are loans and guarantees that become real costs as soon as the borrower (American International Group, for example) defaults on government guarantee, as a co-signer. Consider the recent revelations about AIG.

The U.S. government, in late 2008, "co-signed" $45 billion in a preferred stock deal for Citigroup, and absorbed $240 billion of its losses in the process. Remember, these are just cyclical deficits that pop up in bad times like the one in 2008. Rather, they expose deep structural woes. In otherwords, they are either unable or unwilling to pay for what we spend, thanks to the ever-reliable bond market, which has been able to pick up on our fiscal indiscipline by supplying us with all the cash we need. So if the population at large — individuals, firms, and government together — are not producing and "selling" enough, government's tax revenues from them decline. Alternatively, if government "sells" more than it "buys," budgetary surplus is likely, helping the nation "save."

As for the United States, it managed a surplus in recent times only in and around the year 1999. That came with a trade surplus, too, creating twin surplus (budgetary and trade) positions. The rest of the study period shows a persistent deficit and a deteriorating current-account position: buying more than it sells. As Figure 3.2 demonstrates the United States the worst among them in this regard: selling much less than its peers, and even less so relative to the BRICs. The over-achievers are the key exporting countries that are less dependent on financials — Germany, Japan, and the oil-exporting countries. So here are a few (stylized) facts stemming from the aforementioned identities.

Germany and Japan, which sees the real side as an integral part of national identity, are competitive and tend to sell more overseas. The others tend to pin their hopes rather extravagantly on the bond market (financials) to build domestic capacity. It works to a point but when the bubble bursts, revenue shortfalls either shrink surplus positions or pulls surplus into debt positions, in some cases adding already chronic current account deficit to put public dissaving positions.

Figure 3.2: Growing Budget Deficits

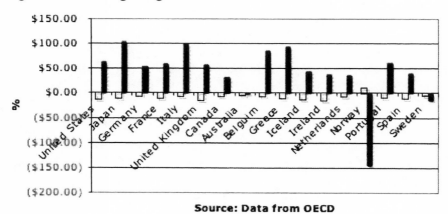

Source: Data from OECD

□ 2010 deficit, % of GDP ■ 2010 public debt, % of GDP

Section 3
The Two Walls that Fell for Iceland, Context of Inquiry: Two Currents

Chapter 4
Nationalism and the Debt Culture

"Everything happens for a reason," or so the superstition goes. So perhaps, it is for a good reason that the two walls came down. Many consumers, at least, see the first wall falling in the goods-and-services sector as a blessing. The same went with the second, until the 2008 financial meltdown. Cheerleaders then, are now filled with angst, unsure as to whether the bond market has the limitless capacity to provide for all the emerging densely populated countries that rely on this market to speed up their transition to matured status, and for the already matured ones that want to have their groove back.

Travelers with Southwest and JetBlue Airlines, and shoppers at Wal-Mart, among others, certainly have noticed removal of the stigma that came with the discount culture. That is, the poor, the rich, and the in-between now take their discount tickets and pick a seat on the plane anywhere they wish to sit, for cheap, of course. This is still the draw. The service is decent, sometimes even great, so is the turnaround time sometimes always, not quite the on-time performance. One could expect such advantages from smaller airlines, but even as they grew larger, such improved performance held up, even driving their more established competitors into similar value-creating efforts. In fact frequent fliers will realize the incredibly shrinking first and business class sections. Literally, the curtains have come down here, and at the financial markets too, only that the societal benefits to are questionable.

Taking a similar discriminatory wall down in the financial sector does not work very well. Insurance practitioners even have a horror story to tell about the moral hazards involved after the teardown. That is, when it comes to access to financial markets, to use a famous phrase, all animals are not created equal. Liberalization under such a lax regulatory environment, the argument goes, could trigger even more morally hazardous behavior, shadows of which loomed in the year 2008.

For the United States, Iceland, Club Med, the United Kingdom, and Ireland — countries that even back in the late 1990s did not have strong current accounts to begin with — it was obvious that because the realities did not allow room for them to grow at an accelerated pace, financials became an escape, and bonds would once again come to shape attitude in the direction of a superstructure. This is the most plausible explanation for why the transatlantic neighbors could choose to cede control of a number of relatively high-tech sub-sectors in manufacturing to emerging countries.

Introduction: Post-War Activism and Fiscal Policy

Economic change comes continuously, and does so unevenly. Policy actions come with a trace of power imbalance, always. Populism, on the other hand, is associated with groundswells of determination to reach the "underrepresented." Fiscal policy comes in handy here because it is particularly effective in targeting such groups and regions. However, if nationalism is anchored in deep-rooted religious, linguistic, and cultural issues, bringing factions on board is more challenging. One strategy with a checkered history is to grant autonomy to a particular group. Regardless of whether such a country becomes progressively rich or poor, over time it will encounter its own nation-building challenges the way Belgium did with the Flemish in the north and Walloons in the south, and by looking at the nature of capitalisms in play ar4ound the world, one can identify the character of activism and related nationalist variants of which the Belgian one is an integral part.

Capitalism is essentially a social arrangement that we commonly refer to as *the market economy.* It has evolved alongside financial markets. What differentiates one type of capitalism from the other, again, is the nature of activism/nationalism and requisite control over financial markets, controls supposed to guide the market toward activist goals, finance being key to matching the means to the set of goals to be achieved.

In recent times we have had as models of capitalism the post-War German strain, other European corporatist types, the Japanese one, the Confucian brand, and the Soviet planning model. Lately though, these lines have become blurred. That was why the 2008 crisis was able to spread so fast across continental divides and across capitalisms, although the Germans and the Japanese, once again, showed some resiliency. But clearly, the capitalisms that took the most hits from the financial shocks did so because the character of activism/nationalism had changed in favor of a supra-national one that we have come to know as "globalization," a capitalism operating from one template.

Growth Poles and Unique Nationalist Forms

Such activism was part of packaged deals that traded during the post-War golden days but even here, there were distinct growth poles. Within those poles and clusters came significant variations driven in part by dynamic fiscal actions. In the United States at least, far from the early 1860s when the 7% income tax went only to finance the Civil War, John F. Kennedy came along to make fiscal policy hip as a developmental tool. He could even spearhead efforts at space exploration, and flirt with cuts too. As a social experiment, the implication was that rather than the government taking taxes from taxpayers and spending it, consumers should do it themselves to, hopefully, achieve the same or even better social outcome. In other less economically developed countries — Brazil, China, Vietnam, India, etc. — a narrow tax base makes public savings a key development tool.

As discussed in Chapter 2, governments accumulate savings by selling more than they buy from other countries. That is why China, India, and Brazil have been in the news lately for selling so much to others, and lending the savings to the United States and the indebted PIIGGS. Such savings from the current accounts are then used to finance development and other infrastructural projects, and borrowed ones in the PIIGGS to finance consumption. This core nationalist/ activist push for fiscal policy among the BRICs and in the PIIGGS shows up in the debt chart from Chapter 1.

Of the little budgetary deficit there is among the BRICs, it can be seen that government spending takes up a large part of total debt as a percentage of GDP. In China, such government spending is hidden in non-financial businesses because most of the relevant bigger companies are government-owned — so it is safe to add both government spending and non-financial business as proxies for government spending. The same goes for Russia.

The opposite is the case among the PIIGGS and in the United States. In the United States, the (Social) Democrats vouch for expenditure increases, as do labor movements, sectoral and ethnic interests. The Republicans go for equally revenue-busting tax cuts, especially for businesses — in good or in bad times, but in bad times states and local governments have to step up with their own bond issues to keep Medicaid, Medicare, higher education, and other essential services running, keeping the bond market very busy in the process. So in good or bad times, the bond market has been indispensable.

Protectionism

Once they had established the social imperatives for nationalism, new institutional formation became the hallmark of the euphoria in newly independent countries in Asia and Africa, especially for the less viable smaller nation states that found it particularly important to build capacity from current accounts on up. That is the developmental aspect. There was even an "infant industry" sweetener for countries to get a growth buzz by changing appropriate relative prices — tariffs/taxes — an idea popularized by Friedrich List, the German-born American economist who in the nineteenth century saw the need for temporary shelter for smaller and "young" economies while they built capacity. By raising foreign prices, they prevented cheaper foreign goods from being dumped on them.

Keynesian Twist

Regardless of the nature of the activist call, I have argued that fiscal policy is effective as an empowering device. If in the form of public works, then it could take a pro-poor or even a (Keynesian) countercyclical slant. Here, fiscal policy is seen as virtuous, of course, if appropriately targeted and effectively implemented. But it is the electoral cycle strand that has assumed notoriety, underscoring what has come to be emblematic of the kind of chronic indiscipline that the bond market ends up underwriting. This (electoral) cycle refers to the use of fiscal policy, in an election year, to finance projects intended to please the electorate even if they are not fiscally desirable. Despite the fact that the jury is out on it as a key vote-getter, it has become a right of passage for ruling parties. A benign twist on this surfaced in the 1990s.

Appropriately labeled *soft budget constraint* in the literature, it was the Soviet Union's long admired tradition of pacifying its key constituency — for managers to "bring home the bacon," to their communities. Needless to say, such an imbalance was a good nationalist price to pay in order to catch up with the West, the insulate *ruble* (currency) becoming the party apparatchik's key nationalist symbol, complimented by a vibrant Eurobond market next door. Put together, this translated into the macroeconomic problem of a culture that had a number of constituents to nurture budgetary deficit. It turns out that Western welfare state countries were as guilty as this erstwhile Soviet Union, but their deficits had as a source post-war macro projects that never wound down, keeping the bond market hyperactive as a sole source of finance. Afterall, political pluralism involves constituency cuddling. Over time, competing demands from these constituencies morphs into entitlement mentality. With no significant source of new tax revenue, budgetary deficit drags on year after year, and as always, as the Constitution dictates, the bond market has a constitutional role in filling in the blanks.

The European Union's Unique Soft Budget Constraint

Virtually all these highly indebted countries in the EU zone have done it all. They were imperial powers, and previously derived most of the net deficit resources from their colonies to power their respective engines of growth, and have been through various phases of growth and development. In other words, they are now "matured economies," perhaps "washed up," one might add. This is where high finance, in the form of the bond market, comes in as a turbo charger of sorts in its capacity as a compressor for forced-induction. This comes in handy, as a key sponsor of the supra-nationalist 16-member EU club that came in force in 1999. Gradually, member states are identifying with these supra-national priorities. Talking about priorities, the European Central Bank sets lots of it.

Its rate of interest was set, for most part, much lower than what would have existed if individual countries had set them by themselves. This is quite a departure from the U.S. model, in that it gave the supra-national feds a monopoly over bond issuance, with flexibility granted to individual nation states to charter their own banks — perhaps an accommodation meant to allow the disparate regions to have their own key financial institutions within the broad regulatory framework set out by their respective Federal Reserves. So, whether with good

(Germany, France, Switzerland) or bad credit (Club Med), all these EC members got the same interest rate. Naturally, with lower prices, economic theory dictates that all agents — including governments, especially those with poor credit who all of a sudden are thrown into a world of money — borrow more and spend more. This is a classic *moral hazard* scenario, a conjecture that has lenders lending to those who need loans the most (Club Med). Having been *adversely selected*, they endanger the rest.

Regional Flavour

Japan has its own thriving finance culture, not a high-finance one, but nonetheless an internal-combustion engine too that worked well with the main engine until recently. There, the high-saving older generation who had long exhibited loyalty to their employers and their government are now at or approaching their retirement/consumption stage. Low birth rates, too, translate into smaller cohorts whose proclivity for consumption threatens the very savings culture that has existed for centuries. The government, in turn, did not disappoint with such savings at their disposal. It propped up activist banks, world-class auto company giants, and other companies producing high value-added exports, all of which contributed in one way or another to productivity enhancement. Like Germany, Japan has a healthy balance of payment even amidst chronic internal financial imbalance. To be clear, such a "deficit" has been a key feature of the Asian Model, and so Japan did not even see this as an imbalance, especially as its capital account held up pretty well.

By lending to countries like the United States (by purchasing U.S. Treasury bills), Japan was doing its own savings, this time in hard currencies, albeit accumulation at a slower rare than the rise in budgetary deficit. So, who will finance Japan's government clientele of corporate giants and generous social programs?

The Japanese are wary of foreigners as financiers, and they do not trust immigrants as the new taxpayers either, which is part of the reason why they resorted to self-help through internal savings. But with a primary deficit of 7% of GDP, time will tell if the debt load of 200% of GDP will dent this belief. A little bit of aside here.

Germany, like Japan, is not quite in the same deficit boat (a mere 4% of GDP), but still has not warmed up to immigration, either. Thus, a modest debt puts it on the path just a notch ahead of Japan on the "payable index," but in fairly good shape relative to virtually all countries in the Euro zone. As for Greece, it follows Japan and Germany's nationalistic zeal, except that its savings and tax base conundrums are much more complicated than those of the two export-driven giants. And as the cost of social programs soars amidst slow growth and much worse public savings numbers, obvious stresses surface, including surging Euro and potentially high interest rates, though for now it is at rock bottom.

All parties — governments, businesses, and households — are in on the borrowing binge. Rather than warn of a looming savings crisis, in Greece, the Kostas Karamanlis government used accounting gimmicks to project a 3.7% of GDP deficit. Of course, no one had an incentive to read much into these numbers until word went around of such understatement. The new Prime Minister George Papandreou did not show any signs of urgency, either, when he took over power in late 2009. As creditors became concerned about the sheer size of the deficit, spread widened considerably, as expected — indicating signs of trouble.

But no matter how Greece got there, we now know that in virtually all regions, simple math reveals that the ratio of deficit to tax base expansion is nowhere near breakeven. It has to be brought in line but in the meantime there is the need for more borrowing from this bond market to quell discontent before permanent funds can be found (taxes and user charges). But before creditors can be assured of payback, they need assurance of cost control, a common practice with bankruptcy cases. This is what the layoffs in the public sectors of Athens, Rome, London, Madrid, and Lisbon are all about, and why poor agricultural producers are up in arms for shouldering much of the social cost since they have to churn out most of the exports needed to pay back lenders.

In the medium term, perhaps the best way to reverse fortune and get the best bang for our buck is via "price" reduction — devaluation of currency. This could stop the bleeding of jobs at home by making domestic goods cheaper for foreigners, but this cannot be done in Greece because the Euro is a regional currency. Even if it could, we know it tends to provoke competitive devaluation by competitors, thus negating the initial benefits.

Wholesale transfers of money (gifts) from well-to-do countries like lender-in-chief Germany also might not fly because the prudent German has a fiscal strain to deal with herself. In the end, fear prevailed. Greece's bad debts were bought (money lent) with a €110 billion IMF loan, but since there was more to come from among the PIIGGS, a different formula was needed to accommodate them all. The €1 trillion fund to be set aside (pledged) on May 10, 2010 by the EU came in handy in this regard. For now, the expectations are that stability is here to stay. But will it?

The SPV Solution: A Panacea?

The bond market is acting up again, this time with a message that the relative heterogeneity of member states requires a permanent adjustment to assure it that they are all speaking the same fiscal language. Remember the €1 trillion fund? The EU is having a hard time raising the money. The idea was to create a special purpose vehicle, or SPV (SPE, Special Purpose Entity, is the name in the United States.). This "special corporation" is entrusted with the responsibility to bail out troubled members. The trick was to buy troubled members' junk bonds, which were to be put in a basket, then issue its own "EU bonds," hoping that a special and narrowly defined mission under the name EU would attract investors in a flash. Another theoretical advantage is that by doing this as an SPV, if it messes up on its "purpose" of bailout, the "losses," as with any other corporation, would be confined to the "entity." So far, however, buyers for these bonds are hard to come by. Rising ten-year bond yields point to continued risk, making it difficult to figure out what interest rate to charge the borrowers.

Chapter 5
The Two Currents, and Responses

Introduction

Especially in the last decade and a half, societies have battled two distinct socio-economic currents. For the agent of interest here, whose adaptive responses in the distant past have tended to take the world with it, the answer is: The social transformational apparatus required to deal with these responses have not come together very well, judging by some unpleasant realities that the aforementioned agent of interest still faces. General Motors Corporation still produces "real" stuff from the real side of the economy, maintains what many see as a sclerotic bureaucracy, but has been toppled as number one in its line of work in the world. More importantly for my purpose, when faced with the Asian real-side challenge earlier on, rather than look inward to adjust and face it head on to shore up current accounts (foreign savings), GM shrugged it off, hoping that financial creativity would save it. In the end, for once, it was disappointed in itself and not with others, as had previously been the case.

The final desperate attempt to save itself was a debt swap proposal to the "owners" — a take-it-or-leave-it proposition. It could not be turned down because the otherwise dependable new bond market could not churn out enough phantom money (loans) for customers to buy its wares — and so, GM could not be saved. Unfortunately, GM's woes are mirror images of America's problems, and that of a few other transatlantic neighbors. GMs financial wing, GMAC, managed to bring home the bacon for a long time but then had to spin off GM in crisis, leaving it to innovate in order to compete, vigorously, in making quality cars. America is in the same bind, having chosen to hedge heavily on financials, and seems to have lost the bet, at least for now.

A decade and a half ago, the disappearance of the Soviet Union had left America at the head of the global household. Now, things are very different. She sounds desperate, in debt, and in need of a bailout, not from the reliable American taxpayer who is now drowned, himself, in (household) debt, but from a new savior identified in a BBC caption as "The Trillion-dollar man" who will save the world.

[1.] This guy leads the poorest country in the group of 20 (G-20). America has no choice but to love her rude banker (China), whose family thrives on calling its own shots and managed to save close to half its income between 1995 and 2005. Not so in America's house. Her total savings rate has bottomed to zero percent, but Hu Jintao has enough saved by his family members (the Chinese people) to be recycled to "Ma" USA through this robust new bond market.

Hu presents two challenges that end up as the paired socio-economic currents under examination here, developments that I contend have stemmed from the giant money mart that "Ma" USA has nurtured actively through her two money departments — the Federal Reserve and the Treasury Department. There was a deliberate easy-phantom-money-creating policy, from which Fannie Mae and Freddie Mac were supposed to translate their (Fed and Treasury) macro vision into micro reality with easy access to loans, especially home mortgages. "Ma" USA will realize, just like GM and its GMAC proxies, that financials are not enough unless she goes back to the real side to produce real stuff, like cars. But GM is doing just that, and so "Ma" USA could very well pull it off in what has become a crowded field of global powerhouses.

The First Current

It is after a crisis that we tend to take stock. The recent (2008) financial crisis prompted us to do just that, in exposing some of our shortcomings pertaining to how we understand the world around us. Combing through a number of these episodic narratives presents quite a bit of intrigue. Mitchell (2008) is one that caught my eye, not as a right-wing defender of the status quo, but as a leftie genuinely interested in tracing an undercurrent: crisis through the lens of legislative initiatives and requisite responses from micro-agents. In his book *Economy: How Finance Triumphed over Industry,* he concentrates on corporate folly in capital structure alteration. In response, consumers are said to adjust their portfolios away from bonds. But the reality is that the lure of above-normal returns, much as it is a key driver of policy insanity, is also tied to the bond market via derivatives and securitizations, which I argue are triggers of such belated responses and consequential crises. In the arguments below, I sketch two key currents (superstructures) that capture most of the cursory narrations presented elsewhere in mainstream literature.

Wave 1: The Real Slide

The first of these two waves managed to knock off snob appeal. Curtains separating first and business classes from economy class in airplanes came down. Department stores including Wal-Mart, Carrefour, the Maxi wing of Loblaws in Quebec, Lidi, Franklins (the Australian discount supermarket/grocer chain), all began boasting of no-frills supercenter discount units — structures that have either replaced or have been forced into convergence with the unique cultural expressions of The Bay, Sears, Bloomingdales, etc. Major airlines joined in, too, and now are operating their no-frills units side-by-side with conventional constructs. Surrogate Air Canada Jazz comes in here for Air Canada; Buzz for KLM; Go for British Airways; Air-India Express for Air India; and Ted for United Airlines. This trend has permitted all income groups to stroll down the isles of airplanes and department stores with discount tickets in hand — and no stigma. It is egalitarian, universalistic, and desirable, one might add. Not so with the second current that swept the financial sector. After all, what is good for the real sector might not necessarily be good for the financial sector.

Wave 2: The Supersize Money Mart

Twenty years ago, 'cybercrime' was nowhere in any dictionary, not even in our vocabulary. Now, cyberspace is where the traffic is, a day-and-night hot spot for our social interactions — and where we do our banking. We also know that where there is money, there are criminals. That is why people rob banks, and why societies struggle to find different ways of dealing with such crime. A second way of dealing with a nuisance like cybercrime is to reverse the trend by sticking with the old ways. The consensus, however, is that we must accept the "globalization" challenge and strike a balance between the old and the new in a controlled fashion. For one thing, the Financial Services Modernization Act of 1999 that formally ended the deliberate New Dealist policy to essentially separate banking and brokerage activities will remain. This effectively ended commercial bank's reign in deposit-taking and in favor of short-term lending, especially in collateralized activities but we did not quite call it that way, though in reality there was one more benefit to The Fed that it could not pass up: lord over only a few monopolistic (or oligopolists) agents in this market while in theory still spiritually tied to the design, under the post-Depression 1933 Banking Act, of recycling money for post-depression economic and social construction efforts. The latter is what we miss, but in comes the exotic new.

Reining in Cost and Ramping Up Profits

Kregel (2010:6) discussed at length how commercial banks treaded "deposit-creation" and "deposit-making" as initiation into the new world of finance. Even with free Regulation Q deposits, he argued, under the Glass–Steagall legislation, commercial banks were in uncompetitive positions because they could not compete with nonbanks, institutions that had the flexibility to develop cost-effective ways of creating liquidity. In fact, commercial banks had to overcome transactional and regulatory hurdles even when dealing with "deposit-making," the art of granting loans through deposit creation. In came structured securitization, another art of laying bets upon bets (financial layering over, say, plain vanilla bonds) on otherwise benign financial instruments. This, in effect, put a damper on system liquidity, thus opening several windows to wide swings in the financial system's stability.

The 2008 crisis happened to expose, in a big way, how tricky securitization of non-conforming subprime as well as Alt-A mortgages can be, in propping up demand and growth. The supply side of the story is what the 84-year-old, 6' 7" giant Paul Volcker weighed in on with his old-fashioned Volcker Rule. This rule did not quite seek to bring back Glass–Steagall in its entirety, but still sought to make separation a cornerstone of a new relationship, helping investment banks or hedge funds keep their winnings and their losses while leaving chartered banks "public" to be bailed out when need be. Stated differently, this rule will limit proprietary trading to 3% of what we call Tier 1 capital.

Volcker knows a thing or two about old-fashionedism. Back in 1979, he was the Federal Reserve Chairman who hiked interest rates into the 20% range (with consequential unemployment) in the thick of the oil crisis. The intention was to quell inflation and it did, but not with voter discontent. The Carter Administration expectedly lost its re-election bid, but Volcker lived up to what central bankers are supposed to do: be wary of politicization of monetary policy. But for those wishing that Volcker would be heard, they would be disappointed. Many investment houses, capitalizing on seeming confusion over market making and prop trading, are merely reclassifying prop traders as asset managers. Having such asset managers enable them take market positions with classification of 'customer-oriented' lets them get away from penalty under the law.

A Demand-Side Caveat

The demand side measures the response to the aforementioned credit incentives, originator being the Fed and the Treasury Department. The brief discussion here highlights what goes on when the bubble is deflated ever so slightly. Recall, on May 23, 2009, President Obama signed a Credit Card Bill that was aimed at, among other things, curtailing unethical reset and excessive interest rates charged to consumers — something that easily makes up the bulk of these companies' incomes. As Post-Keynesian economists say, producers rely on such phantom money to sell to those with such credit trenches. In other words, production decisions are tied intimately to availability of credit, so that our GDP will also be severely deflated when credit is cut. Moreover, such a cut in the availability of credit translates into lower credit limits, fewer purchases, loss of jobs, and declining income. Specific areas of concern for these companies are that:

1. Banks have to reduce, substantially, unsecured lending at a time when dwindling rolls of revolvers (those who carry a balance month after month) translates directly into lower profit margin.
2. Because more people are using charge cards tied to their bank accounts instead of borrowing, again, this move is a profit-buster.
3. A rise in write-offs reduces their margins as well.
4. There has been a rise in unemployment, and derivative "interchange" fees (the charge on retailers using the card facilities).

Put together, these factors gave companies no choice other than to reduce their workforce, and cut back spending in the face of lower profit. This is a credit economy at work, potent in good times, not so good in bad times. That is what "Ma" USA finds herself embroiled in now, unable to unshackle herself from finance and its bubble traits.

Re-Examining the Credit Culture

The context for the study of past crises has been "developmental" in the sense that it has revolved around developing countries. Back in 1998, in a special issue of the *Cambridge Journal of Economics*, leftist economists like Kregel (1998:658), and Johnston (1998) in "Economic Crisis in East Asia: the Clash of Capitalisms," expressed mainstream sentiments to the effect that the crises in Asia are an Asian thing. This 1997 Asian crisis was attributed to the "immaturity" of the South Asian markets in transition to new capitalist forms. But this time around (2008), "immaturity" had disappeared from the discourse because the crisis came out of capitalist titans — the United States and the United Kingdom. "It can't happen here" ended up happening. Even when bubbles surfaced in the financial sectors of industrialized countries (Savings & Loans, Asian Currency fears, real estate) and the real sector (dot.com. and presently sub-prime), we managed to throw in crookery as the sole explanatory variable.

As for the crooks, sure, we have a number of them to point to. There is junk-bond impresario Michael Milken of Drexel Burnham Lambert Inc. fame, who became a household name at the cusp of innovations back in the 1990s. Bernie Madoff, the respected chairman of Bernard L. Madoff Investment Securities and former head of the NASDAQ stock exchange was another. Then we have Sir Allen Stanford, named by the prestigious finance magazine World Finance as the Man of the Year in 2008 for his "innovation" in finance. When it comes to institutions, we have pioneers such as Lehman Brothers, Citibank, Bank of America, AIG and Goldman Sachs. They all made their high-tech mark, but as it turned out, their own Ponzi traps were ingenious enough to sucker in even savvy investors. These included (in the case of Madoff) billionaire Mort Zuckerman, owner of *US News and World Report*; the owners of the New York Mets; the chairman of GMAC; the Royal Bank of Canada, Banco Santander, BNP Paribas, and HSBC.

The danger with concentrating on crooks is that it absolves the massive systems failure that tails along behind our Ponzi mindset. More importantly, from a regulatory point of view, such events and practices distract us from getting to the bottom of our cultural malaise.

Strange Bedfellows

The aforementioned account and genuine attempts at reforms have driven politics to make strange bedfellows out of elites, crooks, and both left- and right-wingers. Charles Ponzi and Karl Marx are the latest celebrities of sorts to join Willem Buiter, a former member of the Monetary Policy Committee of the Bank of England, in a grand coalition at the crisis table. Buiter is calling for financial institutions to be turned into public utilities, seeing as they are quasi-public now anyway, and cannot exist without public deposit insurance. So, regulation is not a buzzword for leftists anymore. Charles Ponzi and Karl Marx would have no problem going along with such calls for much tighter controls on institutions, despite their differing moral inclinations.

As for Ponzi, he would have gone unnoticed in the wave of immigrants from Italy to the United States around 1900 had it not been for a business practice that has come to be known as Ponzi scheme: a promise of significantly higher returns on investments than those of the competition, especially as new entrants pour in. As it turned out, the 2008 experience has reminded us that such schemes are more than the practice of a few crooks. They are part of a broader bond culture, a superstructure of sorts. So, Ponzi is back as an important case study and as a metaphor for what could go wrong as contradictions play themselves out in a number of modern capitalist forms.

Karl Marx is also back in a big way, in the bookstores at least. His *Das Kapital* and *The Communist Manifesto* are runaway hits, well over a century after his death. Recall that the starting point of these books is that "Money is the root of all evil." This is the starting point here as well, in the bond market, where money is literally manufactured, a place awash with good as well as evil. In Marx's days, and even just over half a century ago when the growth locomotive was driven by cheap resources from colonies, and even the military-industrial complex, credit (monetary policy) was the enabler for non-traditional groups intending to access the capitalist dream. Now, it is aggressively more so, a challenge that transformational growth theorists have picked up on.

So, Again, What Happened? The "Berlin Walls" Fell!

The "Berlin Wall" has fallen twice over the last two decades in the United States, with transformational reverberations. The first, as mentioned, was the disappearance of the wall between the debt market and the bond market. The second was the disappearance of the curtains on planes belonging to Southwest Airlines, walls that used to separate first and business class from economy class. The mainstreaming of this discount culture was good for all income groups. "All animals are equal," it seems, a flashback of these good times when, in the U.S., cultural shifts permitted states to provide good quality state universities for students to get good solid education and degrees comparable to the more privileged ones.

The verdict on the fall of the second wall — between the bond and debt markets — is not yet out. But all indications are that what is good for the real side — the Wal-Marts and the Southwest Airlines — might not be good for the financial sector. This is for the simple reason that although it is an important value generator, Wal-Mart is not like our electricity grid, which shuts down our world when there is a major malfunction. But when the financial system malfunctions, it takes the Wal-Marts and the Southwest Airlines with it. That is why we need to scrutinize its inner workings more, and why insurance practitioners argue against a discount financial market, fearing that it is just an invitation for hazards.

Note

1. BBC online edition, 2 April 2009.

References

Johnson, C. (1998) 'Economic Crisis in East Asia: the Clash of Capitalisms' *Cambridge Journal of Economics*, November: 653-61.

Kragel, J.A. (2010) *Is This a Minsky Moment for Reform of Financial Regulation?* Levy Institute Working Paper # 586, 2010.

Kragel, J.A. 'Derivatives and Global Capital Flows: Applications to Asia' *Cambridge Journal of Economics*: 677-92

Mitchell, Lawrence E. (2007) *The Speculation Economy: How Finance Triumphed over Industry.* [NEED PUBLISHER AND CITY]: Berrett-Koehler Publishing.

Panitch, L. "Thoroughly Modern Marx," *Foreign Policy*, 27 April 2009.

Section 4
How the "Pigs" Flew

Chapter 6
How the PIIGGS Flew

The expansive PIIGGS did indeed fly, thanks to burgeoning chartered banks' assets. The three banks of relevance in Iceland had assets worth 850% of GDP (2007 figures); Switzerland has been getting away such bubble for the longest time but the pre-crisis 900% underscored the gravity of the problem; Britain had 450% to contend with, and to a lesser extent, Germany, France, Spain, and Japan, all at around 300%. In the United States, this figure is below 200%. The U.S. number is low because a bulk of the bubble was in the real estate sector so individuals took the fall as well, not just banks. With these numbers, any country could fly up the growth chart. In this section, using factor analysis, I explain how Iceland managed to do just that.

Introduction

The "pigs" (of late expanded into PIIGGS) did indeed did fly, at the back of the bond market, evidenced by its remarkable growth record in the late 1990s. Table 6.1 presents three groups of these countries, the first being a sub-group comprised of the Club Meds — which returned to respectable growth numbers, higher than those of the broader Euro club but not stellar. The second sub-group includes the United Kingdom, a country with a significant comparative advantage in finance. Some countries, Ireland a good example, were able to make up for a lot of lost ground. In fact, for almost two decades, Ireland was the best performer, transforming itself overnight from a country of emigrants to one of immigrants. Now it has gone back to being an emigrant country — its residents fleeing, once again, for greener pastures elsewhere.

This rejuvenation (of the PIIGGS) was precisely what endeared them to lenders - foreign commercial banks. A proxy for this new alliance is reflected in household liabilities numbers presented in percentage as mortgages (chart 6.1 below), and from the Analysis of Variance output in table 6.1, they were not only the over-achievers in this period but also had the widest variation of growth among the group — growth ranging from 8% in Ireland to 1.7 in Italy in the 11-year period starting in 1993 through the meltdown in 2008.

Iceland was positioned comfortably in the latter group, even though it is a natural for the second group, as a resource-exporting country. But it exhibited all the courting traits that others in PIIGGS had shown in the runoff to the crisis. Going a step further by expanding on the Icelandic story in the next chapter greatly enhances our understanding of how such household balance sheet realignment credit, courtesy of the bond market collectively became the new engine of growth.

Net worth, expectedly, trended up among the PIIGGS, and in the United States, so did the liabilities (mainly in mortgages, at well over 100% in the United States, the United Kingdom, and Canada) in the run-up to the late-2008 crisis. No one should be surprised that the crisis took net worth down with it, even as liabilities stayed at pre-crisis levels. In real terms, such liabilities actually tend to go up even more. For example, $100 owned today, with crisis-induced deflation, translates into more than $100 owned tomorrow, part of the reason why lenders (Germany and France, and Japan from the Asian side) had well below 100% liability (60%–74%), strengthening their net worth position relative to their peers.

The second group is made up of the ones to whom traditional growth theories gave room for growth beyond wear-and-tear: Japan, France, Norway, Australia, Canada, Finland, Germany, and New Zealand. These are resource-endowed, export-driven countries (Germany and Japan being dominant among them), countries that have been more prudent and less overzealous in their relationship with the bond market. Nonetheless, had the crisis hit three years later, they would all have been sucked into it in a big way because they were on their way to being self-indulging. This was the case even in the much-touted success story, Canada. It was opening up, a bit hesitantly though, to U.S. banking and household debt practices. Had it not been for the leftist parties (New Democratic Party and Block Quebecois), they would have been drawn into a U.S.-like protracted recession. The two countries being culturally alike when it comes to high household debt would have facilitated this transition. In the end, though, the crisis reminded the ruling Conservative Party (long-time advocates of the U.S. banking model) that the much less spectacular fall of Canada proves the virtues of progressive regulation.

The final group is what I label as "diverse." The surprise member of this group is the United States. It is in this group because despite its high household exposure (chiefly mortgages), at best, it is a marginal member of the PIIGGS. Realistically, however, it is more diverse than the typical slow-growth PIIGGS. The predictable thing about this group in terms of growth is that they are lower overall numbers.

How Bonds Defined the PIIGGS' Identity

One needs to dig deeper into our developmental archives to be able to understand the lure of the bond market, and how modern capitalist and related political institutions have come to embrace it as a key building block, knowing its oddity as one of the few markets out there.

Table 6.1: Variations in Growth: OECD 1993-2004

PIIGGS		RESOURCE AND HIGH EXPORTERS		DIVERSE	
Portugal	2.7	Japan	5.3	Netherlands	2.6
Italy	1.7	Germany	1.8	Sweden	2.9
Ireland	8	Finland	3.6	Switzerland	1.3
Greece	3.4	France	2.2	United States	3.2
Great Britain	3	Norway	3.3	Luxemburg	4.7
Spain	3.5	Australia	3.9	Denmark	2.5
Iceland	3.5	New Zealand	3.7	Belgium	2.2
		Canada	3.5	Austria	2.3

SUMMARY

Groups	Count	Sum	Average	Variance
PIIGGS	7	25.8	3.685714	4.024762
Resource/Exporters	8	27.3	3.4125	1.144107
Diverse	8	21.7	2.7125	0.958393

ANOVA

Source of Variation	SS	Df	MS	F	P-value	F crit
Between Groups	3.85132	2	1.92566	0.990921	0.38874	3.492829
Within Groups	38.86607	20	1.943304			
Total	42.71739	22				

- The bond market does indeed provide a comprehensive intergenerational platform for discourse over all aspects of social imperatives that need a secure financial outlet. This has in fact served as a unifier in many ways, mostly for the good, in a way why it should not be compromised with profit-making agents vying for their own proprietary interests. For example, Trust Fund arrangements were made for our social programs to rely on the bond market as a key investment vehicle. This connected the young to the old by mandating that the young pay for the old in retirement over time (pay-as-you-go). The 401K-like arrangement was an addendum to encourage savers who had reservations over too much progressivity, so that they could save more with less sharing. Employers chip in, too. The state then adds its own contribution, with tax exemption. Under both programs put together, bonds are supposed to be adequately safe havens for us to tuck away most such funds in them. All kinds of institutional investors emerged from this post-war pop culture to fill in

Figure 6.1: Household Balance SheetS: OECD 1997 – 2009

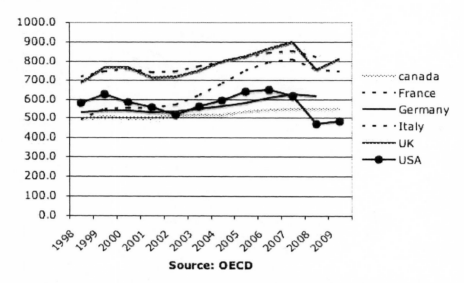

Source: OECD

the knowledge gap of how to multiply the principal and spread the risks over several generations in exchange for a decent return.

• As a valuation method, this bond market might not be able to adequately explain how Tiger Woods' economic value was sliced in half overnight upon news of his personal indiscretions. But it *can* explain, convincingly, why Iceland's value was sliced by over 80% at the beginning of the year 2008. This has other theoretical implications as well. For those who rely on *market-exchange theory* to understand the worth of Iceland, there is the need to seek out the old-fashioned *labor theory of value.*

• The bond market also cannot adequately explain how value can be pulled from under the rubble of Port-au-Prince following the January 2010 earthquake. But we made a case for similar social projects in the immediate post-war era, when bonds were a significant compliment to commercial bank credit expansion activities. To this day, banks are supposed to hold bonds as reserves against deposits.

• More importantly, for my purposes, the bond market — given all the social values listed — can shed light on how economic agents working behind the facade of the market's purity in search of more illusive value could be left vulnerable, seemingly unaware of risks beyond the bonds' legendary "safety." Either way, one thing is certain: The bond market started off as one-stop shopping for all kinds of good social projects. It is where governments secure a bulk of their funds, and get the bulk of their hard currency, by sitting at home and issuing sovereign (foreign-currency denominated) bonds. For consumers, the bond market is a hedge against all kinds of economic adversity. In other words, the bond market has been more than a space for financial instruments to fly through. It is our mental safe haven, and that of our savings and/or investments.

- Proponents of social good also saw, for a while, a coalescence of thoughts on this bond market as a neutral ground for financing postwar reconstruction dreams.

- The same goes with *labor value* theorists. To them, the bond market could be made to yield significant social dividends — at least that was what key political economists like the Scottish Adam Smith, British David Ricardo, and German Karl Marx all thought, tracing value to labor, and focusing on intrinsic-valued items like gold and diamonds, etc., much of whose values are derived from the labor put into them. At the other end of the spectrum are post-Keynesian economists and other *market-exchange* value-creating enthusiasts. This new generation of political economists came to admire the role of bonds in modern finance and in value creation, particularly the art of generating value beyond the convenience of carrying money (the medium of exchange). To these post-Keynesians, money created in this bond market is a means as much as it is an end (in terms of its value). Few trends in the evolution of this thought will be of benefit here.

- In 1989, some Development Economists reached into their toolbox and crafted the Brady Bond. Marketed as a commodity of sorts, this new-age development agent was used to convert Latin America's indebtedness into tradable IOUs. The newly "democratic" Poland in Eastern Europe followed Mexico on a grand scale in another high-profile swap.

- Wherever there are wars, there are bonds to finance them. In addition to adding state muscle to such assurances of financing, Henry Morgenthau, Jr., U.S. Secretary of the Treasury during World War II, was himself given assurances that financial bonds were indispensable to postwar reconstruction efforts.

- For the older generation on the verge of retiring (as explained earlier), expansive government became an extension of a vibrant and emerging welfare state that took delight in its inclusive ideals, as we have seen more recently among the Club Med nations. Thus, Social Security became a convenient compliment to retirement savings, as well as a substitute family. For the ethically edgy, there was a little something in it for them, too. Such savings under pension schemes fit into this schema by drawing the old cultural practice of saving into the new world that was ushered in during the fateful year 1935, when the U.S. Savings Bond was born. Canada followed suit with a "victory bond" to celebrate the outcome of the 1939–1945 war; this eventually came to be known as the Canada Savings Bond. But for those who think all the aforementioned benefits of this market are too good to be true, perhaps they are, considering how we have mixed up our cherished social and private value missions. That is, we have now come to overextend the ubiquitous bond market and rely on it to subsidize our unemployed under our unemployment-insurance schemes; finance job-training programs; provide assistance for our smaller governments; support our anti-poverty struggles; and fund renewable energy and emergency projects, job training, and countless unanticipated social projects.

Warren Buffet's Alternative Plan

Warren, in fact, showed The Fed his way of dealing with the giants in the business. The September 2008 agreement between him and Goldman Sachs underscored his expertise. Warren placed his $5 billion with Goldman Sachs — the new federally regulated bank-holding company. His perpetual preferred shares paid a 10% annual dividend/yield, ten times that of common stock yield ($500 million per annum will be Warren's income). But the downside is that further upside is limited, unlike with ordinary shares (remember, this is a hybrid bond of sorts). However, Goldman Sachs can buy back the shares for a premium of 10% from Warren, at any time. Warren gets guaranteed return and everything else that goes along with a bond, plus a bit more in good times: The agreement provided for the purchase of $5 billion of common stock for $115 a share if Warren so desires, only if the stock price happen to be higher than $115 a share (if the price goes lower, Warren can just ignore it). This $115 is what we call the strike price, an option to be exercised within 5 years of the signatory date.

A similar deal, $3 billion worth, went to General Electric, one of the 10 biggest companies the world. This deal carried a $3 warrant as well, with a three-year buy-back option if the good times roll on, again for a $3.3 billion or 10% premium. Either way, if the stock price rallies, Warren makes a killing. Even if it hit the skids, he still walks away with a guaranteed payback and handsome income to match, unless, of course, the company disappears entirely with little assets to share. Then, Warren will take a hit. Warren's strategy was so impressive that the Obama Administration took a page from it, but without the downside that Warren faced — a sweetheart deal, or so critics call it, a preservation of the status quo rather than a promotion of old-fashioned ideals.

Chapter 7
A Tale of Two Countries: The Icelandic Story

Introduction

Iceland has more to offer the world than the relative monolith of its people, a huge draw for geneticists, even eugenicists. This tiny country, whose population (estimated at 320,000 in 2008) is small enough to fit into a few blocks of streets in Delhi, Shanghai, New York, or London, has transformed the character of its community from traditional to modern, effectively leapfrogging the intermediate stages that had characterized recent development experiences. Certainly, Iceland has proven that it can even ground flights in the Eurozone with its volcanic fumes. More impressive was the lesson in the theory and practice of value-creation that became mainstream read in the last decade and a half, in fact so good at it that it occupied a Top Five spot on the world income chart up until the fateful 2007 year.

Countries of this size tend to have a wide-open economy and for Iceland too, import activity still accounts for a good 45% of GDP. Putting imports and exports together, foreign trade takes up over 80% of Iceland's economic activity. Any attempt at understanding the source of its growth (output gap, for my purpose), will therefore be incomplete until we get a handle on the sources of such growth, an exercise that will be helpful in understanding Iceland's post-crisis economic revival. At the end of the day, it is Iceland's experience with debt deflation and consequential financial crisis formation that I am interested in: a theme that has brought us the kind of intellectual challenge that we have not had for decades. For my purpose, therefore, conducting factor analysis is a key part of coming to grips with events on the ground.

Factor Analyzing Iceland

Iceland's $12-trillion economy (2009 estimate) is no longer driven by agriculture but rather service: 70% of it, to be exact. It is no stretch to say that tycoon Thor Bjorgolfson single-handedly engineered this shift. He did it by shepherding the three dominant banks: Kaupthing, Glitnir, and Landsbanki. GDP per capita and currency strengthened to show their appreciation (fig 1) until late

2007 when both showed severe strain, leaving interest rate to rise to pick up the slack in over-leveraging, effectively putting a brake on most lending activities.

Figure 7.1: Iceland's GDP

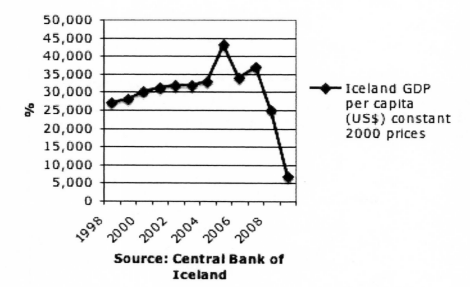

Source: Central Bank of Iceland

Even more so than the Central Bank of Iceland, these banks became the household agents, doing most of the borrowing while still expected to perform their traditional role as savings banks, as havens for pension funds, serve as savings clubs such as mutual funds and investment funds. The central government, amidst such phenomenal growth, made good on its commitment to targeted groups. Student Loan Fund and the Unemployment Insurance Fund were key beneficiaries. Fisheries Development Fund (which guarantees loans to fishery activities) provided for broad socio-economic reach as effective compliments to all these "lending" agencies. Now, perhaps the most important agency to emerge is the National Debt Management Agency, entrusted with the responsibility to numb the burgeoning debt headaches brought about in large part by the Housing Financing Fund (HFF), that organ of the state that legitimized excessive debt taking.

Borrowing trend, expectedly, was across the board. Other than pension plans that experienced marginal growth over the years, all the other potential lenders went big in their lending activities. All of these service (i.e., lending) activities came at a price. It was the almighty crisis that was able to reverse deficit position on the balance of payments, a far cry from the earlier trend of net buying position in buying earlier.

Figure 7.2: Iceland Current Account Balance Percent GDP

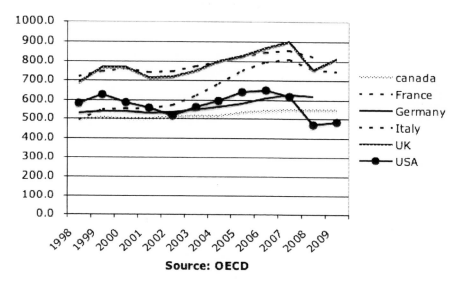

Source: OECD

Variables

The hypothesis here is that deviation of actual from potential is a function of mainly financial factors, of which the bond market is an integral part. Using data from 1980 to 2008, I relied heavily on the OECD data on financial factors, such as U.K. foreign debt, gross national savings, financial balance, and percentage change in household loans. The U.K. connection is of particular importance here in the sense that together withy Netherlands, the two were a key source of growth juice to Iceland as principal trading partners and as lenders. So, it is fitting to assume that expansion of debt there (the bond market) will pad consumers wallet enough to boost demand for debt-led as well as export-led growth. Such openness measures (trade to GDP ratio, current account -1 to 1) are pulled in as structural, much as they are complementary to real-side variables (multifactor productivity).

As opposed to simple regression, common factor analysis (its partner being principal component analysis) comes in handy. Besides being capable of uncovering patterns of connections among all the variables observed, it can even reduce those variables to smaller "common factors" (financial, openness, and real-side variables) based on what it sees as the degree of variance that each factor explains, "rotated" to find connections between such clusters. This shows up as "loadings" with "factors" (-1 to +1), representing the relationship between the factor and the overall factor (output gap; in this case, negative value meaning over-heating and positive interpreted as room to do better).

Table 7.1: Communalities

Communalities		
	Initial	Extraction
Current account	1.000	.863
Multifactor productivity	1.000	.829
Financial balance	1.000	.808
Change in household loans	1.000	.687
Trade/GDP ratio	1.000	.709
Gross national savings	1.000	.794
Export/import ratio	1.000	.553
U.K foreign debt	1.000	.727

Component Matrix			
	Component		
	1	2	3
Current account	.926	.073	.021
Multifactor productivity	.127	.896	-.101
Financial balance	.271	-.116	-.849
Change in household loans	-.572	.425	.422
Trade/GDP ratio	-.820	-.161	.101
Gross national savings	.822	.122	.322
Export/import ratio	.083	.731	-.109
U.K foreign debt	.665	-.301	.440

Sources of Growth

Table 7.1 above (Communalities) shows that 86.3% of variance associated with the current account is shared. The figure for multifactor productivity is 82.9%, etc. Financial balance and change in household loans (tables middle of table 7.1) loaded substantially on Factor 3, with numbers of -.895 and .908, respectively. Export/import ratio and multifactor productivity also loaded heavily on Factor 2 (real side). Lastly, trade/GDP ratio and current account interacted with national savings and foreign debt to load heavily on Factor 1 (openness/outward

Rotated Component Matrix			
	Component		
	1	2	3
Current account	.874	.137	-.282
Multifactor productivity	.080	.906	.046
Financial balance	-.043	.067	-.895
Change in household loans	-.390	.294	.670
Trade/GDP ratio	-.732	-.238	.341
Gross national savings	.882	.120	.039
Export/import ratio	.037	.742	.020
U.K foreign debt	.778	-.328	.115

orientation).

All told, while these three factors explained almost half of the variability in output around potential, it is clear that financial factors (Factor 1) did indeed drive Iceland's growth numbers. A unit increase in this factor (liquidity) drove output to go beyond potential by .474. The negative coefficient implies an overheated economy. The same went with Factor 3 (openness). Trade enhances capacity by .485.

With such robust sectors, it was not surprising that the 2008 financial collapse took these very sectors down heavily: an 85% pay cut (GDP) in early 2008. Agriculture visibly neglected, there was little cushion for a softer landing. Expectedly, the krona collapsed (fig 7.1) becoming literally worthless overnight. But that was just the beginning. Depreciating currency and deflation translates into higher debt obligation, and if there is considerable strain in payment, the financial market's way of punishing such a polity is widening spreads on banks. For Iceland, it was 850 basis points spread, effectively reflecting in reduced lending activities and other gambling schemes.

In the end, in order to stop the bleed of resources going out to finance its liabilities, bankruptcy seemed to be the only option. The disruption in social life in the post-bankruptcy period took its toll on its collective psyche to the point where it needed a referendum on whether to stop paying key lenders in Netherlands and U.K. For those wishing for a Hollywood ending, there was one — a spectacular collapse, and fortunately, a seeming return to prudence that could very well put Iceland back on a more sustainable path to development. More enduring is the fact that this Icelandic experience exposed cracks in the Eurozone countries' financial and growth sustainability.

Certainly, Iceland did not create the Greek crisis, nor did it drive the Greeks to accept more than $110 billion in assistance from the European Union and the International Monetary Fund for the three years beginning in 2010. After all, Greece and its fellow Club Med members are all matured economies that have been uncompetitive at the goods and service sectors of their balance sheets for a while now. Even almighty Japan, long competitive, has a debt–GDP ratio of close to 200% and happens to be situated next to an elephant (China) that has for a decade exported its own deflation worldwide. Deflation in such matured economies, as we know, could be unforgiving to such 'debtor' countries. They get to pay an even heavier debt load because $100 yesterday translates to even more debt today. Reliant heavily on the bond market and on consumer spending, therefore, consumers have incentives to keep postponing their spending, stifling initiatives to jump-start economic activity.

Opening the Pandora Box

Iceland's miracle and the subsequent burst of its bubble emboldened curious market overseers to pry deeper into the books of the otherwise high-achievers so as to expose the shenanigans in (bond) liability management. Again, this is common practice. Borrowers find innovative ways of hiding their liabilities. This makes them look good to stakeholders, and also to financiers who end up showering them with even more money. At the supply-side, the cost of production declines. Put together, from the government to the consumer, everyone is hooked on a debt culture that intimately links consumer demand to cheap financing cost. Greece found itself in this position with its $236 billion public debt load, a lion's share of which is owed to creditors Germany and France. After the Icelandic crash, it became clear that it too had good part of its liability buried under its books.

We have long known that these numbers are questionable, but turned the other way when life was good. That was the source of the ambivalence upon revelations that Greece got savvy accountants to take debt off its books so as to make itself look good, and even packaged the debt to sell in order to raise more funds. That was not all. It also came to light that Greece had entered into derivative transactions with Goldman Sachs. As always, when such "insiders" (banks/lenders) – in this Greece case - bet this way, it raises suspicions that Greece, as with others, had weak spots and so could very well default.

For Eurozone that had hedged so much on its strong Euro currency — key competitor to the United States' greenback — panic set in. Greek Prime Minister George Papandreou had to go globetrotting in March 2010, assuring key lenders that things were not that bad, pleading for speculators to ease off. All of a sudden, the European Union was on Greece's tail, demanding that it expand its tax base from the present 20%, cut spending, and reduce the public sector workforce — troops that represent about one in every three workers.

These days, cuts in expenditures seem to be the only game in town now. Pension benefits are being reduced and eligibility requirements raised; public spending at all levels hit as well. As for layoffs, they are now seen as a socially desirable cost-cutting scheme as agencies seek to balance the public books, so these matured economies, many of which have resisted the lure of legal immigration to bolster a shrinking tax base and for a while now sought refuge in high finance to pick up the slack now faces double whammy. It has to cut expenditure in order to stabilize the financial system, threatening to reduce aggregate demand. No doubt it would be socially disruptive in the shorter run before it gets better.

The Curtain Finally Down in Iceland?

The final curtain has been drawn on the Icelandic drama. Just after Papandreou's tour of the United States and Europe in mid-March, 2010, intended to assure lenders of stability, in a plebiscite, the Icelandic electorate rejected a deal for Iceland to pay off $5.3 billion to investors from Netherlands and Britain, who had apparently seen their investments disappear in 2008. That does not mean that the real credit card bills (debt and deficit) are not going to be paid. Afterall, this is the structural nature of our culture of overspending. Countries now run deficits in the neighborhood of 10% of GDP and still have debts sitting at anywhere from 60% (Canada), 60% (the United States), and 100 for Belgium, and 104% for Italy.

Chapter 8
On Ice: Iceland and Norway, All or Nothing

Introduction

Iceland and Norway are two neighbors populated by relatively homogeneous old-fashioned indigenous peoples - Samis and Norse in the case of Norway and Icelandics in Iceland, and as with many indigenous regions, they have traditionally been big savers as individuals. Governments too followed this script. But underneath this calm, the Icelandics seemed to want to bypass the 1% arable land constraint that had made it almost totally dependent on fishing. They still do. The 1990s therefore arrived on time to upset this tradition. In a way these two neighbors undertook separate paths to creating value the way classical economist like British David Ricardo, German Karl Marx, Greek philosopher Aristotle, and Scottish Adam Smith saw it: that value reflects essentially labor embedded in it.

For Norway, therefore, natural resources would be the anchor. Sure, fishing is always available as a real-side cushion, so are the gold and oil deposits. Norway, perhaps, has more than Iceland. It has the North Sea oil deposits, terrain that spans British territories. Undoubtedly, such specie variation was what drove Iceland to look elsewhere to make up for it. On Norway's part, smarting from Dutch Disease contracted by Holland in the turn of the century, Norway was prepared to stick to the cautionary script. But Iceland was impatient, buoyed by impressive growth numbers (chart 1a below) that put it at par with Norway. It did not matter if it was buying more than it was selling. Thanks to the bond market (securitization) and the phantom money industry, there was credit on demand, almost.

For Norway, in the good ole days when oil prices went through the roof, rather than spend, it saved most of its earnings, used a large part of it to shore up its defined benefit pension plans. The moment stock, real estate, and financial market crashed in the second half of 2008, it seized on the opportunity to scoop up stock and property at bargain basement prices. In fact, while most countries financial and real sides were contracting, Norway had its own boom, for real. Iceland, on the otherhand, like the United States and United Kingdom, represents all that could go wrong in a bubble economy. But don't cry for Iceland.

Figure 8.1: Iceland's Key Financial Data

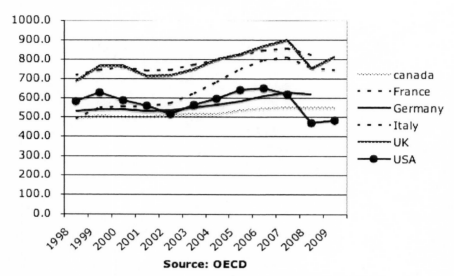

Source: OECD

Shying away from fishing did not work out as planned and despite being, literally, bankrupt, she gets to keep a sizeable portion of assets, and Iceland has a lot of that – infrastructure, human capital, houses, educational and health system etc. But the broader story here is what can go wrong in a bubble economy. So Iceland will be back as a leaner but a stronger country than it is now. Hopefully Thorvaldur Gylfason will put this footnote the next time he turns so bullish as he did on Jan 25, 2008 article *When Iceland was Ghana* that pleaded for African countries to emulate Iceland's example.

Blaming U.K.

More bizarre is the fact that many Icelandic politicians and model enthusiasts did not quite see the model as the problem. They blamed Britain for the most part. Sure, Britain was still a mentor by the year 2008, a friend, a NATO ally, a principal trading partner, a fellow liberalizer, and still the soul of world (Eurodollar) finance. And yes, British bubble too burst at the same time. But since many of the purchasers of Icelandic securities were British and so were in danger of losing their investments, public outcry in Britain managed to pressure the government to use the law with the most teeth, Crime and Security Act 2001, to freeze some of these Icelandic institution's assets as 'collateral', a choice of instrument interpreted as treating Iceland as a terrorist state. To the Brits, they were just after the $30 billion that they lent to Iceland's financial institutions. From the Icelandics point of view, however, the politics of the use of this Security Act overshadowed the deep structural transformation that took its own life after U.S., President Richard Nixon, on a Sunday, August 15, 1971, unilaterally, decided to get rid of gold as a backer of the dollar. Literally, he allowed the printing of notes on demand, dealing a mortal blow to the Bretton Woods system that sought to 'be each other's neighbor' by bringing some stability to capital account.

Robert Reuben, Bill Clinton's Treasury Secretary, followed Nixon's footsteps. He tore down the Glass-Steagall Act in 1999 that had separated traditional (public) banking from investment (private) banking, essentially liberalizing both the current and capital account (real and financial sectors). We know resources of all kinds - goods and lately savings - flow from surplus Asian and Middle Eastern economies to deficit countries. Iceland was not quite a deficit country but it decided, by 1991, with the arrival of David Oddsson of the Sjálfstæðisflokkurinn, to embrace the then standard neoliberal agenda. That freed it to liberalize to be a transit point for such hot global money flows, eventually supplanting the tradable sector – fishing, especially that had sustained it for the longest time.

Tax cuts, auctioning of state enterprises, especially of (U.S.) banks became hip. By 1994, Iceland had upped the liberalization ante by joining the big league of European Economic Area with a severely deregulated financial services industry. Landsbanki **Íslands** and Búnadarbanki **Íslands** readied themselves to morph into the already private **Íslandsbanki**, a bank that itself had come into existence as a result of a merger of a number of other bank. All three eventually adopted the private banking values. Just 3 years later, by the year 2007, leveraged activities from these institutions had reached a whopping 450 percent of GDP in Iceland. One could understand British investor's fury and Iceland's banks (Landsbanki and Kaupthing) headaches. Soon after the crash, the banks were nationalized.

A New Direction?

Using the one nationalized bank as platform, taxpayers resigned to grant key agencies more powers. This translated into three broad lines of policy. Iceland's central bank issued loans to lenders and second, made good on what was due other banks. Finally, counting of the expenses pertaining to guarantees to overseas investors was intensified, especially those to British investors, the largest of the bunch. But this would be tampered by a 'no' result in referendum on whether the British and Dutch residents who lost money in the Icesave Bank collapse should get the $5 billion transfer. Afterall, corporation enjoy limited liability over loses. Why not Iceland?

Why did we not know that Iceland was flying on bubbles?

To be fair, there were signs of trouble but as always, traders, globally, wanted to conduct business as usual with a bit of protection. They took out insurance (mainly credit default swaps) just in case, to the tune of $36 trillion ($22 more in other layered securities), $2 trillion of which were sub-prime (sub-quality) segment. As it turned out, there were considerably more that were sub-prime quality, making it difficult to value them. This is a far cry from the boring low-yield straight bonds that we have long known of.

Creating Value

This section emphasizes how our valuation techniques more often than not reinforces our false sense of security, leaving us vulnerable to the very swings associated with crises that on paper we seek to fend off.

MCI's stock price was at $54 a share; bond rating an AAA. Why $54 a share? And is there any Blue Book (straight line depreciation formula) to refer to for this information? How do we arrive at such Blue Book values, the famous Blue Books being the ones we rely on to buy cars? It will be argued in this segment that the valuation of bonds or stocks measures carries similar emotional baggage in the form of expectations. Not only could such market-exchange methods (of valuing stocks like that of MCI) run at variance with the labor theory of value, but they also seem to be at odds with the intrinsic value that maintains (for example) the value of Dairy Queen. Remember, Dairy Queen produces real stuff with real labor whose value we can measure with reasonable certainty. Not so with MCI or Google. That is why a whole lot of guesswork is needed to make sense of the numbers. That means we are prone to make more mistakes in valuing them — *volatility* of price, as we call it. In other words, will the value of "high tech" Microsoft, Apple, MCI or Google hold up to that of Dairy Queen over time? What is the relevance of earning per share (EPS), PE ratio, or book value (shareholders' equity) in all this? An illustrative example of the vanishing worth of the former CEO of Bear Stearns may be used to expand our practical reach.

For the record, MCI has to do one or more of the following in order to do well at the stock price front:

1. Sell enough of its goods [**create revenue**: price x Q (worth of quantity bought)]
2. Once it does that, it has to manage its business well (keep costs down)
3. With a little cash, or with any gimmick it can muster, MCI can raise its profile (with marketing and image-making so as to convince people to buy into it, raising Q even more)
   - If (1) is looking good, then managing the other two is a matter of discipline.
   - If not, as General Motors and Ford found out the hard way, MCI's fortune sinks fast, the psychological feed taking stock price down with it.

Section 5
Creating Value

Chapter 9
Valuing a Firm, and MCI, Inc.

This section emphasizes how our valuation techniques more often than not reinforces our false sense of security, leaving us vulnerable to the very swings associated with crises that on paper we seek to fend off.

MCI's stock price was at $54 a share; bond rating an AAA. Why $54 a share? And is there any Blue Book (straight line depreciation formula) to refer to for this information? How do we arrive at such Blue Book values, the famous Blue Books being the ones we rely on to buy cars? It will be argued in this segment that the valuation of bonds or stocks measures carries similar emotional baggage in the form of expectations. Not only could such market-exchange methods (of valuing stocks like that of MCI) run at variance with the labor theory of value, but they also seem to be at odds with the intrinsic value that maintains (for example) the value of Dairy Queen. Remember, Dairy Queen produces real stuff with real labor whose value we can measure with reasonable certainty. Not so with MCI or Google. That is why a whole lot of guesswork is needed to make sense of the numbers. That means we are prone to make more mistakes in valuing them — *volatility* of price, as we call it. In other words, will the value of "high tech" Microsoft, Apple, MCI or Google hold up to that of Dairy Queen over time? What is the relevance of earning per share (EPS), PE ratio, or book value (shareholders' equity) in all this? An illustrative example of the vanishing worth of the former CEO of Bear Stearns may be used to expand our practical reach.

For the record, MCI has to do one or more of the following in order to do well at the stock price front:

1. Sell enough of its goods [create revenue: price x Q (worth of quantity bought)]
2. Once it does that, it has to manage its business well (keep costs down)
3. With a little cash, or with any gimmick it can muster, MCI can raise its profile (with marketing and image-making so as to convince people to buy into it, raising Q even more)
   - If (1) is looking good, then managing the other two is a matter of discipline.

• If not, as General Motors and Ford found out the hard way, MCI's fortune sinks fast, the psychological feed taking stock price down with it.

Introduction

Item 1. Apple versus Microsoft

For those who care to find out, May 26, 2010 brought home some happy faces at Apple Inc (AAPL). Apple is now valued more than Microsoft. What does this really mean?

Founded in 1976 and left for dead in 1998, this maker of runaway hits like the pricey ipod, iphone, and more recently, the ipad, made a stunning comeback in a software business that it has shared with competitor Microsoft Corporation (MSFT), founded around the same time (1975). In keeping with the times, Apple does not even refer to its key product as software. It calls it *apps*, a more hip name.

Apple has always had a core following. Its user-friendly software attracted the less tech-savvy users: elementary, secondary, and a segment of university students, plus a few that wanted the cute hardware for (among other things) decorative purposes. That was why users of Microsoft's software ridiculed them as un-savvy pretty-faces. Microsoft, on the other hand, was all business, but then Apple hit the jackpot with a product that was quite unrelated to a computer in the strict sense, but nonetheless an app. Its ipod was a runaway hit, a draw for a younger, mobile generation that has an insatiable appetite for digital music. Overnight, Apple downsized on hardware and concentrated on those apps that got fancier by the day, expanding them into a range of uses — iphone, ipad, etc. For a generation that does not mind spending a fortune on fancy pocketsize gadgets, Apple was just bound to make money, and this forecast of future sales/profit gives it the value that shows up in its stock value.

Naturally, its (market) value would be expected to increase but a 16 fold increase is astonishing - from its 2000 year value of about $16 billion to about $226 billion, a value $4 billion more that of Microsoft if we are to go by NASDAQ's close on May 26, 2010. NASDAQ is the exchange house that trades high-tech company stocks. In finance textbooks, this value is referred to as *market capitalization*.

In summary, this is what Apple has going for it. It has the free-spending younger generations hooked on its gadgets. Thus, even in this crowded field, it stands out out-selling the opposition. The legendary good look now has brains behind it, a perfect combo with the high price to boot, making profit a natural, translated into stable revenue projections, stable profit, and of course, a higher stock price. To get the market value of Apple, therefore, we can add up all the contracts of those who have "lent" money with the hope of getting a bite of that Apple (900 million units of them outstanding), multiply it by the (stock) price that stood at, $250 at market close on May 26, 2010 and we get the $226 billion, slightly more than Microsoft's value of $222 billion, the price tag for a company

(Microsoft) that a decade ago had a market capitalization of double that amount.

A similar measure, although with a slightly different metric, is done annually to get the standings of Major League baseball teams. This is an issue I will explore next, before I get into the more complicated discipline of comparing companies with different characteristics who sell (in)tangibles and cater to a different clientele. Unlike with Apple and Microsoft, valuing companies that sell intangibles (as distinct from, say, iphones) can be tricky. Popular ratios are added to the last section to enhance the flavor.

Item 2: The Value of Baseball Teams

On April 20th, 2007, Forbes Magazine (www.forbes.com) published the annual worth of baseball teams. These "market capitalization" values were based on current stadium deals. So, how much for your favorite baseball team — in my case for my favorite team the New York Mets — and how did Forbes arrive at its value? Simple! It projected revenues less cost. That is, Forbes tried to tally what the baseball teams sell (advertisements slots, tickets) versus what they buy (players' and club workers' salaries, operating costs, reductions in such costs due to tax giveaways by our local governments, etc). If the expected sale of tickets is projected to decline because the team had losing seasons, then expected revenues will decline, too, taking a toll on "profit"/income, and its "stock price." In other words, their "value" declines. As can be seen from Table 9.1 on the following page, the top teams are all popular ones, with loyal fans. They either have won the World Series or have been finalists of sorts (Red Sox, Yankees, Cardinals, Cubs). As a consequence, with their loyal fan base, they sell a lot of tickets and merchandise, creating value along the way.

As expected, such a method of valuation has its critics. Marlins president Avid Samson, for example, is quoted as saying, "As usual, the franchise valuation and operating income numbers are pure fantasy and based on no correct information. To comment on such irresponsible journalism would give it more credit than it deserves." Welcome to the world of valuation: a bit of substance and a lot of style. The point here is that we could be too bullish in projecting revenue, and minimize the reality of unforeseen cost, both of which could go the other way to knock us off the value that we arrive at. However, in the case of Dairy Queen, it could be unlikely that we are too far off because a burger is a burger, and ice cream is ice cream, so we know with reasonable certainty their expected price.

The MCI Love Story

Item 3: Comparing Companies in Different Lines of Work

Back to the art of valuing MCI. What Forbes did with the baseball teams, we can do for MCI, the former long-distance company that was acquired by another telecom firm. This exercise will be like placing four mirrors at each side of a bathroom to look at each side of one's self. For a company as well as a ball team, we can view marketing and other costs to get the total cost picture. On the other

Table 9.1: Baseball Team Value

Rank	Teams	Current value ($mil)	1-yr value change (%)	Debt Value	Revenues	Operating income ($mil)
1	NY Yankees	1026	8	12	277	-50.0
2	Boston Red Sox	617	10	39	206	-18.5
3	NY Mets	604	20	42	195	-16.1
4	LA Dodgers	482	14	87	189	13.4
5	Chicago Cubs	448	12	0	179	7.9
6	Washington Nationals	440	42	27	145	27.9
7	St Louis Cardinals	429	16	47	165	7.9
8	Seattle Mariners	428	3	23	179	7.3
9	Philadelphia Phillies	424	8	42	176	14.8
10	Houston Astros	416	17	13	173	30.2
11	S.F. Giants	410	8	37	171	11.2
12	Atlanta Braves	405	6	7	172	27.6
13	LA Angels	368	25	10	167	-2.6
14	Baltimore Orioles	359	5	42	156	21.0
15	San Diego Padres	354	8	56	158	13.0
16	Texas Rangers	353	8	45	153	24.7
17	Cleveland Indians	352	10	28	150	34.6
18	Chicago White Sox	315	20	11	157	21.9
19	Arizona Diamondbacks	305	7	79	145	21.8
20	Colorado Rockies	298	3	30	145	16.3
21	Detroit Tigers	292	22	73	146	3.5
22	Toronto Blue Jays	286	34	0	136	29.7
23	Cincinnati Reds	274	8	15	137	17.7
24	Pittsburg Pirates	250	15	44	125	21.9
25	Kansas City Royals	239	28	15	117	20.8
26	Milwaukee Brewers	235	13	51	131	22.4
27	Oakland A's	234	26	38	134	16.0
28	Florida Marlins	226	10	31	119	-11.9
29	Minnesota Twins	216	21	42	114	7.0
30	Tampa Bay Rays	209	19	17	116	20.3

side is revenue — from tickets and TV rights, etc. Put together, the net of these two will shed light on its *bond* or *stock* prices. Typically, those with a large surplus of revenues over cost are supposed to have a high bond or stock price. Either route provides us with a reflection of worth. So for any companies out there, if you want to pump up your stock or bond price, just find ingenious ways of hiding the cost, or else ramp up revenue expectations, or both — and the market will respond positively to your needs. That is why, as we go about valuing MCI, it will be bit of substance, theater, and emotions: the romantic story of MCI Inc., looking for love and finding that two is better than one.

It is the story of a beauty, MCI by name, who dumped SBC and got the attention of another, Verizon, only to get even more attention from SBC. A "bidding" war ensued between the two. What "price" for MCI? In other words, what is its appropriate EPS (earning per share) or PE (price/earning)? Whatever the "price," I am not implying that those we fall in love with meet our fantasized checklist — sense of humor, smarts, sensitivity, kind, good-looking, muscular/feminine, nice smile, etc. Paying MCI's stock price does not necessarily imply that our idealized *PE ratio, price-to-book ratio,* and *return on equity* check out, either. Almost always, it involves a measure of intangibles, and invariably, buyer's gut instincts. So, play along with the dry academic checklist here, for a while, as I examine the first move by Qwest, and then that of SBC. For the record, in this soap opera year of 2005, the largest player in the telecommunication sector was SBC. Verizon was No. 2, MCI was No. 3, and then Qwest.

Verizon's Flirtatious First Move

SBC set the ball rolling with a routine proposal to marry the beloved AT&T Corporation, to become the biggest in this line of work prior to the fateful year 2005. The other competitors/oligopolists in the industry did not want to be left out. They wanted to get in on the action, just like SBC, and so they made flirtatious advances toward — of all people — MCI. Who got the "bride," and at what "price"? As we will see shortly, there was a jealous rage that dragged on for months, producing a "price" that some might argue was excessive, but nonetheless a *price.*

Verizon struck first in this shakeout and proposed to marry MCI, believing that its new larger frame could effectively close out Qwest, the smallest of them all — an outcome that would have left only two of them standing: the all-new SBC and Verizon. Qwest, on shaky ground, had nothing to lose. It got bolder, borrowed money — lots of it — and upped the nuptial ante with the hope of making an impression on the "unappreciated bride." Back to the question of "How much should these competitors have offered MCI?" And was there any (emotional) premium attached to MCI? And the lucky one was.....? Well, a bit of a wait will be in order here. Let us take a brief detour by running through some basic value games regarding these two companies, low-tech Dairy Queen and high-tech MCI.

A company might have more than buildings. It might also have a bit of an emotional premium or discount beyond its Blue Book value. This is what accountants refer to as good will, or the intangibles. So:

- MCI's worth sure does involve the sum of the values of its building, somewhat.
- But the most important part is valuing the intangibles. They depend on:

- Emotional highs at a particular point in time (demand side)
- Expertise to deliver goods/services at reasonable cost (supply-side)
- Whether eventually, in the case of MCI, Verizon emerges as one of only two companies in the business, a market structure that will enhance its potential to make even more money in the future.

Which side (demand or supply) is more important in the creation of such intangibles depends on the company's scale of development. A big cap (company) without much competition in the industry usually looks good because the potential for profit could be endless. If it is a small cap, and capitalizes on its strength by way of innovations in management efficiency, then it will make itself known quickly as well. In the next segment, the easier example of Warren Buffet's Dairy Queen is compared to high-tech Google. Then we sneak in MCI as a compromise to finish up the nuptial game.

Arriving at Value for Firms

(a) The Bond route : Rating agencies in the value game
   Who are (credit) rating agencies?
In theory, there are scores of them, but in reality there are three companies that really count in the credit ratings business. These top guns are all public corporations. They are:

- Standard & Poor's, in business for close to 90 years, and a subsidiary of the McGraw Hill group of companies; and
- Moody's, which started in 1909 as John Moody's *Analyses of Railroad Investments,* an annual railroad bond rating report that has now evolved into a full-blown rating company. Moody's is now a subsidiary of the Dunn and Bradstreet Corporation.
- Fitch Group, Headquartered in New York City, is the smallest of the three major credit ratings agencies.
- Then there are privately held corporations, such as Duff & Phelps, and other small rating agencies worldwide.

The methodologies they use are similar, although the first two — Moody's and S&P — have been around longer, so naturally, finance practitioners go with their lettering in the evaluation of a company's reputation. But how influential are they?

The most popular formula for arriving at this is the Altman Z score. Most of the information needed for this formula is derived from the balance sheets of companies. A high number is supposed to indicate a low probability of default (good company), and a low number a high probability of default (bad or "red" company).

$$Z = 3.3 \times [EBIT/total\ assets] + 1.0\ [sales/total\ assets] + 0.6\ [market\ value\ of\ equity/total\ assets] + 1.4\ [retained\ earnings/total\ assets] + 1.2\ [working\ capital/total\ assets].$$

Notice that if the balance sheet entries are inflated or "cooked," they will yield a higher Z, but catching this is another matter. Recall that Enron had a terrific Z that gave it an AAA rating, but then fell flat overnight after flawed entries were identified in its books.

Credit bureaus have emerged as a powerful institution in the value-creating business. Their opinions on firms, individuals, and governments can significantly

Table 9.2: Credit Rating

Credit Rating		
	S&P	*Moody's*
Best quality	AAA	Aaa
High qualtiy	AA	Aa
Upper-medium quality	A	A
Medium quality	BBB	Baa
Speculative element	BB	Ba
Speculative	B	B
Highly speculative	CCC	Caa
Extremely speculative	CC	Ca
Near default	D	C
Default	D	C

affect you. If you manage to get a loan, the interest rate that you pay on your loans will depend on the rate that these credit agencies give you. With good ratings, you get a lower interest rate, a larger amount of funds, and even smaller collateral needed to secure the loan.

For individuals, credit bureaus serve as references for jobs, and for credit of all kinds. Landlords use such references to screen potential tenants. Many employers and all levels of government believe they will find suitable workers by looking at such numbers.

Better credit ratings also create herd behavior. That is, creditors keep showering "good" firms and individuals with funds that in many cases they do not even need. How many pre-approved credit card offers have you received lately, with all kinds of introductory interest rates? If you have not got any, then perhaps you are a new kid on the block, or else you have bad credit, and bad credit these days is a death sentence.

The grades that credit bureaus assign to individuals are strikingly similar, as the table above indicates. The BBBs and up are the graded ones, with high Zs seen as the good ones with low risks. That is why they pay almost zero risk premium $(b(Rm - Rf) = 0)$. This is in contrast to low-Z companies that are categorized as below graded, the ones referred to as speculative or risky. These "bad" companies pay hefty premiums $(b(Rm - Rf) > 0)$.

The theory goes that investors looking for fast bucks should stay away from the lousy/low premium (b(Rm − Rf) = 0 that the high-Z "good" companies offer. These are for "income investors" such as retirees, institutional investors, and scared investors who tend to seek security of their principal, and therefore prefer high-quality, high-Z companies. Among such high-Z issues are:

- corporate issues ("IOUs" by corporations)
- hybrid (structured) brands of IOUs, such as:
- many asset-backed securities
- mortgage-backed securities
- federal agency issues.

Many a time, such companies overstretch themselves by piling up mountains of debt just because they are offered low interest rates. Although such low-low rates initially decrease their cost of production, in the end these rates could come back to haunt them.

(b) The stock route: So, again, what price for MCI?

First, as discussed earlier, a stock certificate is a receipt of claim and worth. As with all values, it can go up, but also disappear in a flash — a story that the then Bear Stearns boss James Cayne (see chart below) can tell better. His fortune declined by almost a billion dollars. Nonetheless, in stable times, stocks could also be a reasonable measure of the worth of the likes of MCI.

Easy come, easy go! The case of James Cayne, Bear Stearns CEO

Just a year before that fateful day in June 2008, Bear Stearns' stock price was around $163 a share, and CEO James Cayne (who had a substantial stake in the company) was worth almost $1 billion (# of shares x $163). By June 2008, it was down to $2/share (# of shares x $2), and all of a sudden Cayne was down to about $12 million — *way* down from almost $1 billion a year earlier. This is value measure at its best.

Whether by bond or stock routes, the following feature prominently in company "price" formation.

Method 1. The old wordy story has it that you can do price formation by comparing the price-to-earnings ratios between MCI and some average in the industry. As the name suggests, we are comparing share price to annual profit/ earnings. It makes sense because your worth depends on how much you make, or for MCI, how much it makes by way of profit/earnings. If it is too high, then you are paying too much (stock price) for the profit, and if it is too low, you are paying too little.

Method 2. involves the use of present value of cash flow. This formula, stated below in the box, extends the familiar cash flow (profit) method with an investor getting cash flow in the form of dividends, representing a share of MCI's profit by virtue of the stock contract. If you had given out that money in the form of bond purchase, the cash flow would have been interest/coupon payments. At 6%, a

$1,000 bond will bring you close to $60 per year ($1000 x 6%).

Technical terms to remember
Present Value =   Future Cash Flow

(1 + Required Rate of Return)^{Years one has to wait for the cash flow}

It should be noted that this (present) value depends on a bunch of "ifs" as to whether money will be flowing beyond the present time. Thus, MCI's (stock)

Figure 9.1: Bear Stearn's CEO James Cayne's Worth

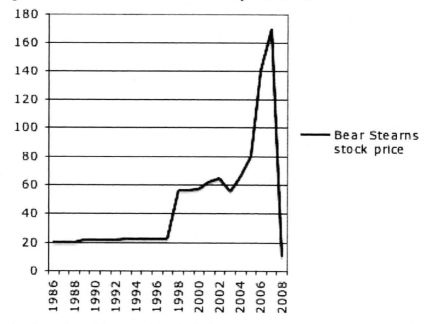

value depends on (a) competition in the industry that MCI is in; and (b) the market for what MCI sells. As a matter of fact, it depends on a whole bunch of other things as well:

- Its assets
- Whether these assets are going to diminish or appreciate in value over time
- Potential earnings, which in turn depend on whether the industry is a growing or a dying line of work
- Potential earnings elsewhere (opportunity cost)
- Whether MCI has good competition in the industry, and if so, how intense it is, and what the competition is worth
- Perception of worth

As you will notice, all these factors have big "ifs" in them: a matter of psychology that, in turn, has large effects on market behavior, making accurate measurement difficult. But that is what finance is all about. So, back to the fight over the bride, MCI. The nature of the substance and the fluff with respect to her "price" will become clear. Whether this "price" is worth it is up to you to decide. Whatever your take on the matter, sit back and enjoy the fight between Qwest and Verizon, over the bride, MCI.

Table 9.3: Qwest versus Verizon

QWEST	VERIZON
A CLOSER LOOK • Smaller player • Growth (stage 2 or 3) company. Does not pay dividends. • Does NOT have a "high-tech" wireless wing • Shares traded for less than $4 (see chart) traditionally, considerably lower than normal for a firm in a takeover bid, as of April 2005 • Market capitalization about $7 billion, less than the $8.9 that it wants to use for the acquisition • Intended to borrow (leverage) for buyout, a sign of easy credit and "irrelevance" of "cost."	A CLOSER LOOK • Pays dividends • Has a "high-tech" wireless wing purchased from Qwest • Shares traded at about $34 as of April 2005 • Shares traded for considerably more than $4 • Minimal leverage
Why court MCI? Marriage of convenience/desperation? 1. With 15.5 million residence customers who are disappearing by the minute, it needed MCI's customers 2. With only $2 billion in cash, it would have been be unable to compete head-on with either Verizon or SBC in the laying of fiber optic cables for TV in residences 3. Marriage sought to define who actually is a big wireless or land-line player	Why court MCI? 1. Gets one more telecom company out of business and off its back, so that it could be dominant 2. To legitimize its dominance after a few scandals

4. Potentially serves to make up for the "high-tech" sell-off of its operation to Verizon. Getting MCI puts it in a competitive position with Verizon and SBC — a surprising turnaround considering that Qwest was only born in the 1990s during the high-tech era. It then crashed and was kept on life support by old-timer USWest, which it bought for $41.5 billion in 1999.	
5. $14.8 billion in savings, mainly from job cuts	
6. Wants MCI's $5 billion in cash and cash equivalents as a cushion for its $17 billion debt	
7. Growth prospects as the largest telecommunications carrier	
8. Use of its cash flow to pay (Qwest's) debt.	

Round 1: Verizon's proposal

On Valentine's Day 2005, Verizon sends a proposal to marry MCI. Bill for the wedding party: $6.7 billion.

Round 2: Qwest's jealous rage

Offer

- Qwest offers $8.9 billion, a day before April Fool's Day 2005, over $2 billion more than Verizon's bid. This was 35% more than its (Qwest's) market capitalization, obviously an eye on a 40% stake in MCI.
- MCI was to own 40% of the MCI–Qwest merger, compared to 4% for Verizon's proposal for an MCI–Verizon merger.

Qwest's options

Let someone (a proxy) pick up Qwest's cause: Verizon hoped that unhappy MCI shareholders would be hostile to MCI's management for opting to marry Verizon. In other words, Qwest wanted the Verizon takeover to be declared hostile — as in a "hostile takeover," that is.

Round 3: Counter-offer

MCI is to acquire a 13.4% stake, and buy off the Mexican billionaire Carlos Slim Helú for $1.1 billion — $25.72 a share in cash for his for his entire 43.4 million shares, payable in a few weeks, making Verizon the largest shareholder of MCI.

Round 4: MCI shareholder revolt

Helú got a higher price for his stock, to be paid in a couple of weeks, but other shareholders were promised 66% in cash at $23.5 a share, payable about a year after regulators signed off on the deal. Obviously, the other MCI shareholders were not happy about such price discrimination in favour of Mr. Helú, and threatened revolt. Qwest made such a revolt worthwhile with its own "final offer" of $9.74 billion in cash and stock, or $30 per share — a $2 billion difference versus the one Verizon offered MCI. In addition, Qwest promised to put away $1 billion in "comfort money" to allay the fear that there was no competitive fire left in Qwest.

On April 24, MCI's board declared for the first time that Qwest's bid, worth $23.10/share, or 30 percent more at $9.75 billion compared to $7.6 billion from Verizon, was superior to that of Verizon. Now, Verizon had until May 3 to come up with a counter-offer, or permit MCI shareholders to vote for either of them. Notice, it is shareholders, not management, who would do the voting.

Round 5: The final chapter

Verizon moves, and finally closes the chapter.

On May 2, there was word that MCI's board of directors had voted to accept yet another sweetened Verizon offer, 13% less than that of Qwest. The details were as follows:

- $26/share, up from $23.10/share comprising $5.60 in cash and the rest in stock (they would issue their own stock to replace MCI's).
- Verizon would guarantee MCI's stock value, and ensure that stockholders could take advantage of a stock price rise between May 2, 2004, and whenever the deal was finalized.

Verizon's offer was lower than Qwest's $30/share. In other words, $8.5 billion in cash and stock, still less than Qwest's $9.85, but considering the promises made by Verizon, that was good enough. After that, Qwest angrily withdrew its offer, ending one more soap opera of corporate takeover.

- In September 2005, Verizon became deeply involved in Fios TV service delivery — optic cable that brings TV, phone, and Internet service — even though it was not making money on it. But because the competition was offering similar services, it decided to join in.
- A footnote: On June 4, 2008, Verizon adopted Alltel for about $28.1 billion, turning herself into the largest cellular telephone provider, with "Ma "ATT taking the second spot.

Further options for Verizon

- By way of procedures, Verizon had to declare that it could not beat Qwest's offer. Under this scenario, MCI would have to compensate Verizon by $240 million for breaking the deal sketched above or come up with a counter-offer. But Verizon did not need to worry about that.

Where Does This Patchwork of Theories on Worth Fit In?

After enjoying a taste of this soap opera about a takeover, and derivative value determination driven by emotions, we revisit a patchwork of theories that have been a staple for many investors. These theories generate psychology-free "hard" numbers consisting of ratios from financial statements. When interpreted carefully, they can make some sense as to the sustainability of cash flows, in effect giving us a clue as to future profitability and continued strength (or the lack of it). Many of these ratios are presented below. Overall, however, it is the manager who is the point person for value-creation projects.

1. Value through financial ratios, for all firms.
2. The ratios

$$EPS = Net\ Earnings/\ outstanding\ shares$$

EARNINGS

1. EPS (Earning Per Share): is simply a measure of earnings/profits. If earnings are impressive, then chances are that the shareholders out there get a share of it. But, as it turns out, this measure of profitability has some pitfalls.
    *   There are three kinds of EPS.
        *   Trailing EPS points to the previous period's earnings
        *   Current EPS points to the current (forecast) earnings
        *   Forward EPS points to future EPS
    *   The "value" of a company that issues a lot of shares (outstanding shares) declines
    *   It is difficult to compare, using EPS, across or even between firms in the same industry.

All these things have to be put together in order to make sense of any EPS figure.

$$P/E = stock\ price/EPS$$

1. Price to Earning ratio tells you how much is being offered for earnings. A high P/E ratio is either a sign of promise, OR, if this value is extremely high, an obvious a sign that the stock is overpriced. Be careful about using P/E religiously to evaluate companies (such as Google) that do not have many physical assets, as they tend to have low values.

Non-earning figures

$$P/B = share\ price/Book\ Value$$

1. Price-to-Book ratio (P/B) gives market value in relation to book value. As in the case of the earning measure, a lower P/B ratio points to potential value. For instance, if a company has 20 new cars and a competitor does not have any, the former will have a higher P/B ratio. Companies like Google that have mainly skilled workers to show for themselves will have lower values, which could be misleading. So, the following observations about P/B can be made.

- Since B depends on hard assets, it is most useful for evaluating companies with hard assets. Thus,
- because it ignores intangible assets, it will not be particularly useful in evaluating the worth of the Googles.
- It understates the assets of leveraged companies. Here is how. Highly leveraged companies — such as cable and wireless telecommunications — have higher than normal P/B ratios. Assets = liabilities + owners' equity, and so increasing leverage increases liability, thereby decreasing book value of assets. B is reduced in the process, which increases P/B. Companies with successive losses as well could have negative P/B, rendering interpretation suspect.
- A low value is seen as a sign of no confidence, or representing an undervalued stock (growth company, or a possible "buy"), while
- high value, obviously, while a sign of strength, could also be a sign of an abnormally high stock price. A high P/B that can be matched up with high ROE tells a better story of health, while a large difference between the two is a warning sign. For example, a high P/B and low ROE could point to an overvalued stock.

2. Return on Equity (ROE): A word of caution here with Return on Equity. It is possible to use accounting manipulations to reduce the denominator (book value), with schemes such as:

$ROE=Net\ Income/book\ value$

- write downs, and
- stock buybacks
- as a way to push it up. A case study is provided below. Checking out such things over a longer period of time gives a clearer picture. In good times there is a kind of trickle-down of prosperity. That is, ROE rises when the economy is generally good and the social pie increases. The article below tells us a bit about this, with the resurgence of growth companies in good times.

Security Market Line as Storyteller for Firms at All Stages of the Industry Life Cycle

Much has been said about the so-called security market line (SML) as a forecasting device. It is used to tell a story about the value of a typical firm, irrespective of where it lay within the industry life cycle. Other stories can then be told of how, for the consumer, a little bit of risk-taking with their cash, could yield handsome payoffs (value/premium) of the type b(RM + RF). For the firm, such risk tells of its position on the corporate growth chart. Growth firms, for instance, pay a hefty premium for "borrowed" funds, because such firms are infants with an unknown future. This is not the case with mature firms, known quantities that take up their positions near the prestigious risk-free level, giving them a sense of control over cash flow (earnings). Let us treat of each of the three groups of firms in turn.

The Value Game

Valuing Warren Buffet's Dairy Queen, and Warren himself

Warren Buffet is a very popular billionaire. Of course, if you are a billionaire you will be popular, even if you are not likeable. People are intrigued as to how you got your billions. But Warren is known to be more than a moneymaking machine. He has a unique moneymaking philosophy of *buy-and-hold* that runs counter to the present, day-trading-like philosophy of investments. His belief is that intrinsic values are just that: If the value of an investment goes down it is a buy signal, and holding it will eventually pay off when price surges. Unlike some billionaires, he not an arrogant person; in fact, he is extremely polished, polite, and easygoing, and has a stereotypical, gentle Midwestern demeanor that makes him an interesting study. This entrepreneur and financial genius, who was consistently the richest person in America before Bill Gates bumped him to second place, still preaches simplicity. He advises people to bet on old-fashioned companies that produce simple items that are held together by intrinsic values, such as his own low-tech Dairy Queen franchise, the famous ice cream retailer. And the last time I checked, he was still staying in the house that he bought in the 1950s.

Determining the Value of a Company Like Dairy Queen

- If sales can be predicted with reasonable certainty (earning certainty), and
- With fewer expenses, we get bigger profit/earnings, and earning prediction is what Wall Street is all about.

Earnings tell a story of how much the company can spend, save and invest, or pay out in dividends. If we take into consideration the nature of the competition in that industry, we can come up with an earnings picture over a period of time that amounts to value, in this case the value of Dairy Queen.

Buffet also is in the insurance business because, again, he says he knows what he is insuring, and in the insurance business the only surprise is whether an "accident" arrives today, tomorrow, or the day after. Such events trigger payouts. Fewer such events translate into less cost relative to pay-ins (premiums), increasing earnings and company *value*. Let us now evaluate Google.

Googling Google's value

Unlike Dairy Queen, if you google, Google for its value based on its predictable cash flows, you will likely come up empty. Why? Google does not quite use the Jetta car or truck that Dairy Queen uses to run its errands, so valuing it is an art rather than a science. Yet, as of year-end 2006, eight years after the company was born in a Stanford University dormitory, Google's stock value topped $500 per share, a long way from the $85 IPO in August 2004, catapulting its worth to $163 billion. At that point it was worth more than the combined value of McDonald's, Du Pont, and Anheuser-Busch, and second to Cisco Systems Inc., the Silicon Valley giant. But we hardly know what Google really does, other than the fact that its management seems to be thinking on its feet, as they only release bits and pieces of information about its strategy. We do know the following:

- Google is primarily a search engine. By search engine, we mean that like Microsoft, Yahoo, and AOL, it is an electronic search conduit around the globe for all kinds of information.
- As an e-mail provider, it operates a blogging service, and develops software that accelerates web traffic.
- We also know that Google sells advertising space that is displayed alongside search results and other online content, but since Google does not produce original content, we cannot technically refer to it as a media company.
- It wants to become a digital library, with an eye on being in video and delivery of messages to mobile computing devices. That has taken it to the point where it now has a 5% stake in AOL/Time Warner, and has taken over You-Tube.

As with many others in the high-tech business, it has a much younger founder, in fact two of them. In a way, these unique co-founders seem to be doing most of the advertising for it, just by being who they are.

Their unconventional management style, and a mystique of rock-starish proportions, provides all the intrigue that one would wish for. This "boy company" that we have heard so much about deliberately keeps the financial community in the dark on its future and earnings picture, a practice that keeps the company's mystique going. It is not quite a rags-to-riches story, but certainly Sergey Brin (with American-born Larry Page), an immigrant graduate student then and now worth well over $16 billion gives us the classic immigrant success story. Both are hot on the heels of Bill Gates for personal worth supremacy.

What we do not know is what they plan to do next, other than compete with Microsoft on operating systems and a do-it-all browser. For a while, an eBay-style electronic payment system was also rumored to be in the works. It may very well be that the Google guys themselves do not really know what is next, but realize that the suspense is generating even more interest than the service they are selling. This is much like a groom or bride to be who fears that settling down will expose his or her vulnerabilities. Staying away from the matrimonial obligation here is just the right strategy to keep premiums up. Simply put, there seem to be something sexy about not knowing what exactly one is doing. Just a vague description and some proof of capability is enough to keep the money rolling in. For gamblers who bet on such companies, even if they lose big, the treat of betting on such an exotic makes "no pain no gain" worthwhile, and for now, they do not have to worry. It is all roses at Google.

So, back to the original question of Google's worth. Certainly it is bigger than competitors Yahoo and eBay combined. To insiders, it is even bigger than all the

Big Ten media giants other than General Electric. How did Google's stock get an $85 price tag at its debut in August 2004, and rise past the $460 mark as of August 2009, less than 6 years after going public?

Answer

1. Potential (intangibles), in addition to the little things listed above: search engine, etc.
2. The investment bank hired by Google to offer its stock for the very first time (Initial Public Offering) could help out, and they did. Their trick was to price Google's profit/stock in such a way that if Google had seen itself as a future star, then the price could be high enough to get some money now for investments, so that it could share the profit with investors/lenders later. A target kitty of, say, $500 million could then be priced either as $5 a share to reach as many people as possible (even those with shallower pockets), or $10 a share for those with deeper pockets. Notice that there is no difference between the two prices. The stock at $5/share yields $500 million (100 million x $5/share = market cap[italization]). The $10 per share (50 million x $10/share=$500) gives the same $500 million.

Sometimes the offer price is less that the market/book value. If this happens, then it is viewed as under-priced. How come? Sometimes people might not appreciate the worth or the "beauty" of a company — its intrinsic value, including brand name, trademarks and copyrights, unique labor force, etc. These values are difficult to figure out, as was the case with Google. That is likely why its stock value went up considerably after the initial issue.

So, when it came down to it, Google Inc., with earnings of $712 million on revenue of $2.6 billion in the first 6 months of 2005, even managed to price a follow-up stock offering on Sept 14, 2005, with 14.16 million shares priced at U.S. $295 — a slight discount from the previous market value. Interestingly, Google did not pay dividends, although its market value at this time was a healthy $89 billion, based on the 292.8 million shares expected to be outstanding after the latest round of offerings.

So, how much is MCI Corporation worth?

So far, in the discussion around Dairy Queen, the emphasis has been on "real stuff." When it came to Google, something real was being offered, but there were other intangibles that we did not really understand. Yet these carried enough weight to yield a handsome premium before and after the initial issue. With MCI, we get both: some real and a little bit of intangible/premium — a middle ground, so to speak.

Two measures have traditionally been used to assess such value. We can:
   •   Look at the company's bond rating. This is a relatively imprecise

measure because it gives a sense of the company's direction but not its entire worth, as is reasonable given information that is out there.

- We can also look at their stock price and what underlines such a price: potential earnings. Recall that the stock price times the number of shares out there gives you a value/capitalization.

On paper, the second (stock price route) tends to be closer to reality. On the other hand, stock is subject to wide swings in price; it could be worth $1,000 today and only $45 tomorrow if bad things happen to the company or if the economy tanks. But market capitalization and bond ratings usually to go together. Better bond ratings are usually accompanied by soaring stock prices. We will further examine both of these strategies.

Chapter 10
Valuing Petro-Canada and Other Quasi-Public Enterprises

Introduction

Who is better at creating value for society: government-run or "private" corporations? In general, it is not an easy question to answer. But given the social imperatives in Canada back in 1975, then Canadian Prime Minister Pierre Trudeau thought the government, in this instance, and in some critical sectors, could be the better hands-on value-creator. That was the main reason why he created Petro-Canada. Three decades after Trudeau, this culture of hands-on "parenting" has slowly given way to a "rent-a-parent" model that I will get to shortly.

Theoretical Justification for Petro-Canada's Birth

Why create Petro-Canada, when Trudeau could have allowed the "market" to do its job unhindered, letting private companies spring up to take care of all kinds of business? As his first reason, he cited national security. The energy sector, he argued, was of significant national security and public concern enough to warrant public action against the dominant U.S. oligopolists and their subsidiaries that had dominated all spheres of the Canadian economy at the time. From an efficiency point of view, therefore, he saw Canada's energy sector as being too critical to let the private sector oversee it. The private market, from this vantage point, "failed" because individuals were consuming too much energy in a way that led Canadians to rely on the United States to pick up the slack. This had created a dependency relationship. Trudeau's famous speech[1], reflected that bias: "Living next to you [the U.S] is in some ways like sleeping with an elephant. No matter how friendly and even-tempered is the beast…one is affected by every twitch and grunt." Petro-Canada became a symbol of the Canadianization exercise.

There are even better cases that demonstrate why governments find it necessary to step in rather than let the private sector run the show. That is, in some activities, it is difficult to identify the benefits and costs to others, or to exclude others conveniently without incurring significant costs. We call such goods and services *public goods* and *services*. By way of an example, one cannot have a personal police force with the full powers of a cop, nor can one rent-a-cop from a private company precisely because the government is assumed to be better at it, for free and for everyone. And governments are supposed to be able to screen personnel better, and prevent ex-convicts and "Rambo" cops from taking over this all-important public function. So, to encourage the spread of the benefits of law enforcement, governments limit the private market in this sector in return for expansion of the public domain.

A Case of Pure Public Good

Public goods' benefit/cost goes beyond the individual
  Market failure is inherent in both public and private goods. It is the failure of the pricing system to capture all the costs/benefits to individuals that apply to the larger society. In fact, as goods move from public to private, new forms of "failure" emerge: pollution and social dislocation a few of such by products.
  Characteristics of public goods
  • Non-excludable — it is difficult to prevent one from accessing them. They are expensive to provide — for example, police services — but the benefits spill over beyond their impact on one person or a few people. Finance comes from general revenue.
  • It is difficult to know when and how much of it you will need at a particular point in time.
  • Benefits run across all social and economic groups (non-rivalrous).
  • Governments tend to have monopoly over their provision.
  • Roads, fire and police services, and pre-university education are examples.

Someone threatening you? No problem, call 911. It is free, courtesy of the taxpayer. No one is excluded. But once such advantages of the public domain are lost, then a rent-a-cop franchise can emerge. We have already seen a trend in the emergence of relatively sophisticated private eye (investigating) companies, security companies, and, more importantly for energy production and distribution, the emergence of Petro-Canada as a "private" company. Better yet, there are:

Quasi-Public Goods: Intermediate between Public and Private

Companies under government control — for-profit or not-for-profit — are called Crown Corporations in Canada (after the Queen of England's crown, of course). Governments underwrite them from general revenues. The extent to which such corporations can be moved into the private sphere depends on the degree to which they have the flexibility to exclude. That is, whether they can impose user charges at reasonable collection cost without needlessly discouraging use; if so, then they are good candidates. Now, in fact, the most exciting companies listed on stock exchanges are the ones that were just recently converted from "public" to "private." As examples, Canadians have Via Rail (railway transportation),

Air Canada (air transportation), Business Development Bank (the promotion of investments), and Petro-Canada (production and marketing of gasoline), companies that made such a transition from Crown Corporations to quasi-public ones. They represent the private sector doing some significant "public" as well as "private" good. The government is on standby to bail them out when necessary.

Such a (quasi) public goods sector is very fluid. Over time, as market conditions change and governments become increasingly unpopular, the private sector is called on to fill in the blanks. Fortunately, there are a few Bill Gates around now who can afford to buy them, and even buy smaller countries if they so wish. A few other arrangements are intriguing, too.

The mail delivery segment of Canada Post is still wholly public, just like the United States Postal Service. Canada Post's courier divisions are for the most part privately run, in competition with private sector giants like UPS and FedEx.

In the case of public broadcasting, the Canadian Broadcasting Corporation (information assembly and delivery) can be compared to its sister organization in the United States, the Public Broadcasting Service (PBS). What is the difference between them? The Canadian one is fully funded, but the American one relies on government grants, which are supplemented by "pledge week." The USA has other quasi-public arrangements such as Fannie Mae and Freddie Mac, the mortgage-lending giants that acts like private companies. They were recently taken over by the government, following the 2008 financial market meltdown. All these arrangements point to a lot of changes since the nationalization culture of the 1960s and 1970s, in Canada and elsewhere.

Characteristics of Quasi-Public Goods
- They are largely services
- *Exclusion* is possible but not perfect, because there is still spillover of costs/benefits
- Delivered mainly by oligopolists
- Benefits could be reduced when congested
- Rationale behind delivery is the promotion of specific goals/objectives
- Parks, garbage collection, colleges and universities, transport are a few of them

---

Petro-Canada, from (quasi) public in 1975 to private in 2004
Catalysts of change

1. The Soviet Union had disappeared, and China changed from a command to a mixed economy. Petro-Canada could not avoid the cultural shifts that had been sweeping virtually all countries.

2. A salient feature of this anti-government culture was reported inefficiencies in such quasi-public agencies, and Petro-Canada suffered the same fate. Horror stories such as the Auditor-General's report in Canada and cost overruns made Crown Corporations unpopular, creating a backlash that prevented the privatization culture from taking root.

3. (Private) oligopolists had become so big that venturing into traditional pubic domains such as hydroelectricity, natural gas, roads etc. had become just another walk in the park.
4. Significant infrastructure emerged by way of regulatory arrangements for the private sector to fill the government's shoes with respect to controlling the likes of Petro-Canada.
5. Private benefits and cost over time could be adequately separated so as to warrant private control, despite some imperfections.
6. New ways of delivering services have emerged. Internet-based interactions have surely been an efficient document delivery mechanism to rival the giants such as UPS, FedEx, USPS, Canada Post, and government information delivery systems.

Now that they are almost fully private, what are Petro-Canada and China's State Grid Corporation worth?

Let us stick with Petro-Canada for the moment, but extend the analysis to China's utility giant. For starters, we have to try to put them on the market to figure out what offers are out there.

Problems with valuation of (quasi) state enterprises

1. A rap against such companies is that cash flow to the sole shareholder (government) would be a prime source of macroeconomic and business inefficiencies. It can even work to suppress potential true values. That means such companies, arguably, could have more value than we place on them now.
2. Political interference and negative perception on waste and inefficiency further dampens their true value.
3. Counter to these points above is the fact that such (state-run) companies do not adequately reinvest in their businesses. When matched up against the fact that such reinvestment in listed companies shows up in useless mergers and acquisitions, whether they are private or public, it is difficult to get the true value of companies in general.

Yet, we still find ways to value them. Back to Petro-Canada's value.

Word had got around that Petro-Canada was on the chopping block back in 1990, with an IPO in 1991 and a secondary one in 1995. By July 2001, the first shares had been sold at $13 each. How did they arrive at the $13? This is not real science, but a little bit of art will point to clues.

Some methods of valuing (quasi) state enterprises

1. Lines of work like utilities or energy have very few companies in them: one, a couple, or a few more. To get a feel for their (stock's) worth, one has to compare (Petro-Canada's) potential stock price to that of others in

the business, if there happen to be any "private" ones out there — such as EnCana (privatized energy-producing wing of the Canadian Pacific conglomerate), Shell, Imperial Oil, etc. That is one way to get what we call *market capitalization* (price of the share times the number of shares outstanding). At the time when Canada's Liberal Government announced its intention to sell off its 19% share, Petro-Canada had 50 million or so shares in the hands of the public. Knowing the price therefore make it easier to determine the value.

2. With market capitalization at hand, underwriters can go to work to market the financial papers, and there are companies in the business that do just that: Merrill Lynch, RBC, [PLEASE SPELL OUT] CIBC Wood Gundy, Citigroup, Merrill Lynch, etc. They make pitches to potential buyers, many of whom are institutional investors like pension funds. Such investors/buyers will state the amount of stocks they want to buy and the price they will be comfortable with. This is the source of demand for the stocks.

3. Then we come to the supply of funds for the company. If the government wants to own part of such a business, it buys into it and lets the rest go to individual investors. Alternatively, if it is totally privatized, then private investors — both domestic and foreign — scoop up the government's share, taking 100% of the total offer.

   In the case of Petro-Canada, by the end of the April 2004, and before the secondary offers, price gravitated toward the $64 mark — a similar rage to that of competitors EnCana, Shell, and Imperial Oil. This is supposedly Petro-Canada's value.

4. How far will these worldwide shifts toward the private end up going? Perhaps they have a bit of a way to go. In the meantime, Exelon, a private company in the United States, has now turned out to be the biggest such utility turned private company — a feat that only big governments could claim prior to the 1980s. With such shifts come complaints about various levels of "market" failure, leading to calls for — once again — expanding the range of the public domain. Was Pierre Trudeau right after all in his fears about private market dysfunctions?

Purely Private Goods

Private goods are the goods we buy at the store: oranges, iphones, bottled water, TVs, jeans, etc., all of which have the characteristics sketched in the following table.

Table 10.1: Characteristics of Private Goods

	Excludable	Non-excludable
Rivalrous	**Pure Private goods** Soda, clothes, ipads, cars	**Common-pool goods** Health Care services, fish in ocean, wood in forests
Non-rivalrous	**Club Goods** Cable, satellite TV, universities	**Common Resources** National defense, unconjested non-toll roads, weather information, public libraries

It is labeled "excludable" because if I do not have $1, then I will not get a bottle of water from a vending machine, but if you have $1 you will. Thus, consumption is *rivalrous*. If there are no bottles left, your having that bottle prevented me from enjoying it. By way of government control, apart from safety rules that governments set, private agents who negotiate the price of both inputs and outputs carry out production and distribution.

Does this mean that in the provision of purely private goods, the market does not fail? No! As a matter of fact, as goods move from pure public to private, a new set of market failures creep in. That is why a little bit of vigilance and oversight by the government is needed to assure buyers in their decision to buy water, pizza, coffee, or energy.

Note

1. This quote can be found in en.wikiquote.org/wiki/Pierre_trudeau

Chapter 11
Valuing Governments

A Country's 'Value'

By now it is clear that adding up Warren Buffet's expected income, and like incomes from all workers gets us GDP, interpreted as the money that a country makes in a period of time, usually a year. Thus, if GDP grows consistently, especially in a non-inflationary manner, theoretically, that country's worth increases. If it decreases consistently, then it is worse off. Better yet, if such worth comes from tangible assets rather than paper money, then a $100 today will likely be close to $100 next year so such a worth comes close to the intrinsic value ('actual' worth). I demonstrated earlier how financial measures of the value of Iceland, USA, and the U.K. did not stand the test of time in the runoff to the 2007/8 crisis because a chunk of their worth came from paper money. Not Norway. It did not fall for this financials craze to the extent that others did in large part because a barrel of Norway oil coming up for sale will likely hold its price next year too than say the stock value of MCI. Generally, GDP increases when the following supply ingredients improve: if *Potential GDP* increases from:

- Population increase. A good educational system determines the magnitude of labor available to work for this national pie to increase
- Productivity boost. This is a sign of how efficient population does things, in turn dependent on innovations, technical absorptions capacity, and degree of human investments in skills and tertiary educational, and to a lesser extent the good-old physical capital investments.
- Awakened entrepreneurial spirit
- New resources discovery. This gives the population more to work with.
- Discovery of new markets to sell and buy goods.

Blending Supply- and demand sides: Broad Measures of Government Value

One key measure of value that phantom-money-creating agencies look for as a measure of value are the following.

Leading Indicators

As the name suggests, *leading* indicators 'leads' us to think that things are looking up, or down. They are not measures of value in themselves but are pointers to potential directions of value: reference point(s) for comparisons. Key among these indicators are *consumer confidence, orders for plants and equipments*; *manufacturing orders*; or *stock market* figures. We also have a class of indicators that we call lagging, meaning such variables lag economic activities. For instance unemployment lags economic activities because as the economy starts doing well, it takes some time before producers are confident enough to start hiring (lagging decision), and for out-of-job numbers to start going down. I do not treat them exhaustively here. Instead, a bit of emphasis is placed on the all-important leading indicators.

What goes into leading indicators

Consumer Confidence

Consumer confidence indexes merely reflect our mood. They can point to some good things to come but could also be false alarm. The consensus on its credibility is that it does well at predicting turns (cycles) in the economy but not really what to expect in a shorter or longer-term horizon. In otherwords it is a gauge of popular sentiments in a foreseeable future.

The University of Michigan has been a pioneer in this consumer-oriented *Consumer Sentiment Index*, supposedly a predictor of consumer purchasing plans for the next six months. With consumer spending roughly 70% of our economy, our mood has a psychological effect on producers because the latter bases their production plans on the former.

Producer's have their own index. Their mood/index is measured by Conference Board's *Consumer Confidence Index* (CCI). If both Consumer Sentiment Index and Consumer Confidence index trends up, then we know consumers could be feeling really good and willing to spend, and producers willing to hire. If they trend down the opposite effect is likely: gloom as cautious consumers scare off producers to cut back production activities, including layoffs. But notice, such feel-good could disappear with the least sign of distress, shaving off a large chunk of financial assets but not Norway's oil value.

Stock price averages

The second leading indicator discussed here are stock price averages, on paper a measure of the value of firms. Since people own such contracts and can cash them in, when such values go up, GDP also goes up, and if companies profits goes up such values will likely go up as well. This implies we can pay more taxes to governments for their own values to go up. Put together, that is why adding such company's worth/index sheds light on a nation's value. What I do next is to formally derive such numbers.

We divide this aggregate worth of the Warren Buffet's Berkshire Hathaway and other companies by a number (divisor) to arrive at a familiar average/number – index. A summary of the main averages/indexes - DJIA, S&P, Nasdaq, and Wilshire 5000, and some around the world - are presented below. Notice, increase in such indexes are just on paper: paper money, that is. That is, the Dow could be worth 10,000 pts today and drop by 40% tomorrow, just like that.

Index #1

Dow Jones Industrial Average (DJIA)

Charles Dow, in 1882 gave America and the world a number – a Dow average, this number was supposed to reflect the worth of 12 big public companies that at the time were so hip that they were driving (high tech) actions - transportation companies the most dynamic and profitable among them. They helped open up the hinterland in the West, South, and North. Over time though, with the industrial revolution came big industrial companies, that rendered these transport companies relatively redundant. As a result, on May 26th, 1886, Dow split transportation from industrial firms. The industrial firms segment then came to be known as the Dow Jones industrial Average (DJIA). Again, a higher one tells us of whether we are gaining value, a lower value a potential loss. Thus, DJIA:

- Represent 25% of the value of the total market
- Only $7 billionaires (in annual sales) need apply. Though still very popular as a theatre, it is the other indexes that are heavily used for theoretical and practical work.
- Price rise of higher-priced stocks, using simple arithmetic averages, raises the value of the index more than an equivalent rise in the price of lower-priced ones
- only 30 of the elite companies that trade at the New York Stock Exchange (the auction market), excluding transportation and utility sectors, are handpicked by editors of the Wall Street Journal to reflect he character of the industrial sector.
- Composition of firms rarely changes, though over time as the economy undergoes structural shifts from agriculture to high-tech. as a consequence, companies have been moved out and others into this elite club of 30. In fact apart from General Electric, none of the old guards remain in this club of 30. With over 10,000 public companies, no wonder this index is ridiculed for not being representative of the real America or the real world.
- Price weighted in the sense that a $1 change for a $20 stock has the same effect as a $1 change in an $80 stock.

Calculation of Index

We can simply define the DJIA, like all averages, by adding up *prices* of company's stocks divided by the number of units. So a price aggregate of say

1,000, divided by a Dow divisor, say 10, gives us 100. What will happen if one company tries to make its stock cheaper and more affordable? We call it stock split. If this company's stock price[1] was $100 and was split 2-for-1, its new stock price becomes $50 (times 2 gets us the original $100). The new index will be 950/10 which translates to an index of 95, which creates the impression of a change in value when in fact nothing has happened other than a split. To correct for this we change the divisor to 9.5 that gets us 950/9.5=100, the original value.

Here is a complete example[2]

Table 11.1 Price-Weighted Index

Companies	Market price (*base period* Jan 1999)	Market price, *current period* Dec. 2005
A	$4	$10
B	$5	$20
C	$10	$40
D	$12	$45
E	$15	$8
Total	$46	$123
Average Price	$46/5=9.2	$123/5=24.6
Index = $24.6/$9.2 x100 = 2.67x100 = 267		

Index #2

Standard and Poor's 500 Index (S&P)

S&P is the most admired index just because it occupies the middle ground of all the indexes. It represents roughly 70% of total value of the market. And as the 500 suggests, it uses 500 of the widely traded stocks picked by S&P board, with a bigger 'weight' placed on larger corporations. That is,

- if a bigger company like Wal-Mart's stock price value changes, it has a bigger impact on market than a smaller one.
- The requirements to be part of the S&P are to be worth at least $4 billion with four consecutive quarters of profit;
- liquidity by way of 0.3 (of value traded/market cap); public float at least 50%.
- In short, S& P is
- Value-weighted index (not price-weighted as Dow Jones) meaning market value of a company gives it the weight in the index
- *Average value* of the stocks of the *widely held* companies, making it a *weighted index* because it takes into account (weight) the number of shares that people have out there. In fact apart from DJIA that is price-weighted, all the other indexes are value weighted. The problem with the S&P is that even though it is much more inclusive than the DJIA, still, only forty companies still represents more than half of the index's value

Calculation of Index

Table 11.2: Value-Weighted Index example 1

Companies	Shares outstanding (in public hands)	Market price	Total value	Weight
A	1,000	$10	10,000	1.5%
B	5,000	20	100,000	15%
C	10,000	40	400,000	60.5%
D	3,000	45	135,000	20.4%
E	2,000	8	16,000	2.4%
			661,000	99.8

Index #3

Nasdaq Composite

- Launched in 1971 by NASD, it has more stocks in their index than the Dow or S&P 500.
- It consist of all the stocks (over 5000 of them) traded at Nasdaq but weighted more toward the so-called new-age (promising) tech stocks, over 4,000 of them. As a value (capitalized) weighted index, each company weight is consistent with the market value. The problem with this index is that tech is always a fashion and fashion comes and goes. Thus it is more volatile than the S&P or the Dow.
- Thus, it does not claim to represent the 'market' but it keeps us informed on directions in the tech tector.

Calculation of Index

Stock-split: Share B splits 2:1

Table 11.3: Value-Weighted Index example 2

Companies	Shares outstanding (in public hands)	Market price	Total value	Weight
A	1,000	$10	10,000	1.5%
B	10,000	10	100,000	15%
C	10,000	40	400,000	60.5%
D	3,000	45	135,000	20.4%
E	2,000	8	16,000	2.4%
			661,000	99.8

Apple's 2-For-1 Stock Split

Apple Computer Inc, in February 10, 2005, through its board, authorized a two-for-one stock split . in so doing, it increased its authorized share count to 1.8 billion from 900 million. Thus, each share that was held by Feb. 18 attracted additional share.

Index #4

The Wilshire 5000 Total Market Index.
Represents all the 6500-plus firms that trade in the United States. But such inclusiveness end up being a disadvantage too because only a few of them make up a bulk of its value. It also does not reflect foreign companies.

Value Line Index
Value-line is an equal-weighted index comprising of 1,700 companies from the NYSE, American Stock Exchange, Nasdaq and over-the-counter markets.

Indexes around the world
- France has CAC 40
- Canada TSX
- Germany DAX
- Japan Nikkei
- Britain FTSE 100

Problems with using stock prices as a measure of value

Make no mistake about it, if you own a stock issued by, say, Microsoft, you own a piece of paper, a claim to your share of Microsoft's profit. But this is just paper money that could be worth, say, $5,000 if you sell it today. But by tomorrow, just a threat of lawsuit against Microsoft could sink the value to close to zero, a story that Canada's Nortel Inc.(NRTLQ) knows so well of. Its own value sank to pennies after being the best high-performing company that every pension fund held as a safe haven stock for over a decade. On January 12, 2009, it filed for bankruptcy protection against creditors. From this we can see that such volatility makes this *market-value theory* of value unreliable in some instances. Gold's value, in contrast, is stable because it supposedly reflects mainly labor put in it with little emotions built in. This is the *intrinsic value* that we have heard so much of.

Housing starts
If people are buying the most expensive asset in their life – houses - then the economy should be doing well. And if the economy is doing well then firms that build such houses should be making money as well. Stock prices follow the same script. It creates capital gains. The economy follows with impressive growth numbers, making us feel even more confident to spend more. Thus, housing start's upward trend 'leads' activities.

Factory orders
Similar to housing starts, the more orders firms place, the better the chances of sales and profits and so the better the chances to add to their worth, their stock

value, and to GDP.

Retail sales

Higher retail sales suggest that people are confident in the economy and are spending.

Notes

1. This example is from Investopedia's tutorial '*Calculating the Dow Jones Industrial Average*'
2. This is a modified version of a problem Hirt & Block's Fundamentals of Investment Management 6th Ed,1999.

Reference

AOIFE WHITE (2009) "EU presidency: US stimulus is 'the road to hell'" Yahoo news, Mar 25.

Chapter 12
The Asian Challenge and Responses from the Real Side of Market Economies

Introduction

It is an undeclared war, an unwinnable one. That is why the U.S. has not openly declared it. Afterall, it is just a challenge, an East Asian challenge, broadly defined as a more proactive government that manages to expose U.S.A.'s lax approach to governance.

There are variants of this Asian Model ranging from one-party, authoritarian, and even multi-party strands, all driven by social innovation, monopolization, and drive to maintain social order. They do, in fact, exemplify social and economic policies there. Juxtaposed to the more reactive one in the 'democratic' United States, the Asian model, however defined, has presented more than enormous challenges for curious leftists who saw it, at one point, as just another variant of the famous a Keynesian big G (as in government expenditure). Its resilience in the face of crises has undoubtedly been successful at numbing epithets that portrayed it as incapable of transitioning beyond exports. It is clearly an exemplar of what a state should be, at least at a transitional stage. Even the 'weak state' variant in Japan has done very well.

Not fancy, just effective

Made in Taiwan, Made in Singapore, Made in Hong Kong, Made in Czechoslovakia, Made in Korea, and now Made in China have all been sweet rewards from this East Asian model, admired as effective in generating growth even if not beyond exports. Leninism was not quite this all encompassing but was also grounded in such discipline, deriving most of its *surplus* from forced industrialization, a transformational sweetener from the real side. Under both models, financials and non-tradable sectors were not revered. Rather than appreciate such virtues (of proactive government), neo-liberalism gained added notoriety in re-branding it as *financially repressed*, though virtually all development experiences point to it as the best architecture that guarantees a relatively trouble-free development for countries at such transitional phases of development.

Alice Amsden, in numerous writings, referred to such 'progressive' schemes as 'getting prices wrong': for producers, and for selected consumers to get protection (subsidies) at transition times. In return, companies had to conform to and not resort to 'unauthorized' capital transfer otherwise they faced jail time, even death penalty. Consumers got their share too. Price ceilings on a whole range of consumer products became an essential anti-poverty staple. A few more of such 'wrong prices' are listed below.

'Wrong' prices
1. As with all industrializing countries, low, low wages, and subsidies (wrong prices) become layers of insulation that helped tilt investment and trade in their favor. Such wrong processes were indexed into favorable exchange rate as well as long-term interest rates. In brief, these countries strived to:
2. Nationalize banks. Korea and Taiwan held the key to this by aggressively following the footsteps of Japan. Backdoor nationalization comes in here via close association with governments, banks, and corporations. The Nissans, Toyotas, Hyundais, and Kias have all been cited as exemplars.
3. Tweaked interest rates: In general, Asians created three-tiered interest rate structure:
   • The typical discount rate
   • real interest rates on foreign loans meant for preferred firms in specific industries were consistently negative in the sense that with high inflation and fixed exchange rate, negative rates became the inevitable outcome
   • other rates

Conglomerates

The anchor to monetary policy (wrong prices) was the institutional construction called zaibatsu (Japan), chaebol (Korea), and los grupos (in the case of Latin America). They were carefully constructed to either compete or develop other lines of price advantages beyond the traditional edge that low-wage provided. Interestingly, these countries did not derive the spin-offs from developing modern technologies from the ground up the way their predecessors did in the West. They merely took advantage of the post-1944 Bretton Woods culture of fixed exchange rates to design capacities of all kinds as anchor to their own full-employment policies.

A step-up in such 'wrong-price' scheme was monopolies (conglomerates). Unlike the anti-trust drift in matured economies, monopolies were encouraged here to compete with the more established western giants. Afterall, they were taking a page from the West's industrial policy manual that Alexander Gerschenkron popularized. So the Tatas, The Hondas, The Toyotas, the Daewoos, the Hyundais the Embraes are all here, from the same region acquiring pieces of conglomerate behemoths like Jaguar Motors, Hummers, the Pontiacs etc. they are even leading the world out of the global recession.

Chapter 13
When the Old Become Hip Again

Introduction

The proverbial Wall Street tradition is rich. Take whatever part of it you like and chances are that the famous NYSE and NASDAQ across the street from each other on this street will be part of it. One might even throw in the famous brand name banks associated with it. Wall Street is a part of the Manhattan Island that derived its might from a military wall built by the Dutch to fend off the British in the 17th century. The finance part came to being when, after these skirmishes in the 18th century, 24 of the most influential brokers emerged with an idea to trade securities on the space that we now call New York Stock Exchange. Transformed into economic wall and even extended to the middle - what we now call Midtown – Manhattan is now a peaceful corporate wall in the Big Apple, appreciated more by tourist now than by those making corporate deals, a sign that the Street has departed from its ideals as progressive corporate innovators and instead devoted its efforts to promoting its elitist fraternity.

The internal pressures on it reflect its psychological deflation. The corporate lifeblood of previously high-flyers like the GMs and the Kodaks has taken a toll on it. Part of this shift is a sign of the time, but there is a genuine undercurrent of structural shift that is rattling this once almighty Street. One measure of it is to glance the skyline that defined the entire southern end of Manhattan Island. You will notice that it has been dwarfed by even more magnificent conglomerate of buildings in, surprise, the developing world where cities like Dubai, Shanghai, Rio de Janeiro, Mexico City, and Kuala Lumpur, spaces that have real people producing real stuff from the real side are on its heels. But substantively, to reiterate, Wall Street still has one thing going for it. Imperfect as it might be, imperfect, it is the proverbial 'free market' spirit of corporate finance has followed its long established peace after skirmishes a couple of centuries ago. As the discussion below will show, the very basics of this long tradition (of finance) need to be revisited.

Private (family) control vs. Public Money: *Buffet, Conrad Black, the Swede, and The class of Bs*

I have always been a fan of the so-called Swedish model – virtues behind 'Class B' shares. That is why the Lord Conrad Black's story, depressing as it might be as a counterweight to this model, needs revisiting, aware that Warren Buffet's presence looms high.

In Warren Buffet and the Swede's worlds, life is about families, and some of these families are 'more equal' than others, exactly why we have preferred shares: for holders to get a first shot at dividends and at liquidation. For the ultimate in control, such elite families corporate loyalty becomes more than remote control stock ownership (Class A). These elite Class B shareholders thus have more at stake than financial interest.

Reward for owning a stock

1. dividend (regular payments) and stock buyback
2. capital gains (change in the value of the certificate by   the time you sell it).

Types of shares gives an indication of how far in the distributional chain the particular stock is on – treasury, authorized, restricted, and outstanding. To show where true control lies, such differentiation presents a sense of how far 'Swede' or 'American' the corporate culture has gravitated to.

$$\text{Control} = \frac{\text{Treasury} + \text{restricted} \ \times 100}{\text{float}}$$

The larger this control value, the more control the company has over itself. Conversely, the lower the percentage, the more control outsiders have over it. Lower percentage means that outsiders can buy shares from the public, which can lead to takeover. Tag on the politics of control from which share types (class A or B) provides, and one has an idea of the kind of (im)personal corporate culture at play. Either way, *class* and *types* of shares are intended to align incentives so as to encourage stakeholders to do what is right for the pocket book of all parties. This is where the 'lender' gives up guaranteed payback of principal in return for a form of voice - directly or indirectly through the election of a management team. The latter has been blamed for the bastardization of the American model. The Swedish one, on the other hand, seem to be the favorite that Buffet and the Google guys, and judging by their unique arrangement for control, they have hitched their wagons to a personal touch by these very 'lenders'.

Technical terms to know

Voting Shares: A holder of a voting share is entitled to vote for delegates – board of directors and enact laws governing the company (with few exceptions).

Figure 13.1: Types of Shares

Authorized — Usually decided once you go public. Number can be changed over time.		Shares outstanding — Outside the firm's control.
	1. Treasury Kept in a lockbox, a guard against (hostile) takeovers.	
	2. Restricted Sweetners by company to management/employees. Need clearance from SEC because of unique ownership arrangements.	
	3. Float In leveraged buyout managment target this in tender offer (generous compensation) to take company private, in many cases to the displeasure of shareholders.	

Non-voting share is the converse – not voting rights.

Class A shares: shares that usually carry no voting right. In mutual fund context, carries an initial sales charge – popularly known as a front-end load, paid the very moment you buy into the fund.

Class B shares: Generally offered to employees. In mutual funds context, it is the kind of (pooled) mutual fund shares that attracts commission (back-end load) when you sell it. The longer you hold class B shares the smaller a commission you are charge

Advantages of Class B shares

Permits founders/families that started the company to retain extra power either because they see such elite groups as better than the ordinary (class A) stockholder, or is intended to prevent (hostile takeovers (we explain it shortly) is a way of transitioning into a 'public' company. founders are supposed to have a longer term view than Wall Street, and since such class-B shares cannot be traded, it provides a safety net for long-run planning Sometimes the control of the capital permits such privileged group to channel resources into areas that a more 'public' company cannot.

Though an engendered species, the virtues of this Swedish model is in large part why the NYSE is careful not to dilute the power of class B shares, the key corporate fixture in Europe. Perhaps sensing its virtues, NYSE preference seem to be to issue new ones with even better voting rights, even price them based on the privileges that they confer.

The more liquid the non-voting shares, the lower they are priced than the class B (privileged) premium ones. It should also be noted that with voting shares comes wider bid / ask spread, meaning that if you buy it you will have to pay the 'sticker' asking price but then you lose if you sell it at a lower (offered) price.

The Conrad Black story points to what could go wrong with such premium shares. Insiders in this company arrogate to themselves the power to use public money anyhow they sew fit. All in all, it is in finance that we can say with reasonable moral certainty that discrimination is desirable, and that class B shares is still in.

In other words, there are some holders of shares with first shot at profits. In fact there are ones with:

- (dis)proportionate claims/control over residual profits as well as
- influence over decision-making.

In his Berkshire Hathaway Inc. family, for instance, Warren commands (with a class B share) a majority 1/30th interest compared to A-class shares that carry 1/200th of the voting power. The Ford family is another example. With just under 4% of the total equity in the company, it has a dual-class share that permits it to have a 40% stake (voting power). Do not confuse this class of shares with *types of shares*. Google is in the same elite club. Like Warren, Sergei Brin and Larry Paige also have class B shares, claims that confers more power/control than class A shares. Likewise Echostar Communications. Its founder and CEO Charlie Ergen has 5% of the company's stock but a super-voting class-A shares with a whopping 90% of the vote.

Companies issue stocks to different clienteles in large part because:

1. it wants to prevent hostile takeovers: buying up a company's share outstanding and trying to take over even though management opposes it.
2. use stocks (treasury) for future use to buy another company rather than rely on debt.
3. If float is small and catches the eye of investors, this might drive up the stock price significantly, making it over-priced relative to earnings and other key performance measures
4. Similarly if investors lose appetite for the stock, with even small float means they will have a problem selling them, pushing price down even more than the 'fundamental' numbers suggests.

Lord Conrad Black, at the helm of Hollinger's International[1], controlled all of the company's class-B shares: 30% of the equity and 73% of the voting power. He was accused of running the company like his personal property by misusing the compensation process. The end of the story is now a familiar one – collapsed stock price, eventual felony conviction and his July 2010 release. As a privileged class B shareholder, the rap was that he used his power to steer capital to finance his lavish spending through various companies that he indirectly controlled (20% of it). Despite Black's indiscretion, extra power for family in a number of cases

Table 13.1: Examples of Companies with Dual Control (as of September 2007) and the Controlling Shareholders

Examples of companies with Dual Control (as of Sept 2007)			
	Market capitalization $bn	% of market capitalization	% of total voting power
Google	141.4	26.0	77.9
Comcast	81.4	0.3	33.3
Newscorp	73.2	32.3	100
Viacom	27.7	8.6	100
Ford Motors	14.8	3.7	40.0
Wrigley	13.8	21.6	73.4
Hershey Company	12.6	25.4	78.2
Controlling shareholders			
	% voting power (as of Sept 2007)		
Sergey Brin, Larry Page	57.5		
Brian Roberts	33.3		
Rupert Murdoch and Harris Trust	31.2		
Summer Redstone	72.3		
Contey and Charley Ergen	95.8		
Ford Family	40.0		
William Wrigley Jr.	31.1		
Two Hershey Trusts	79.8		

are warranted so as to permit bold productive (long-term) experiments.

GM Joins in

Though many people did not quite understand the character of the debt-equity swap that GM offered on that fateful June 1, 2009 when it filed for bankruptcy. The objective was for GM to shed its debt and not be obligated to pay it back. Trading such obligation (debt) was for a crack (for lenders) at 10% of the profit that GM makes. This means if GM ends up losing money or disappear from the face of the earth, then, of course, 'lenders' lose big. But if it makes money, then both parties win: GM makes money and lenders take a cut too. This is the plain vanilla version of debt/equity differences that corporate America clearly seem to have moved away from into reliance on this giant securitized money mall, a cultural shift that stifles incentives for stakeholders to stay involved in day-to-day administration.

Note

1. Companies in it including Sun-Times Media Group as it is called now with holdings including Daily Telegraph and the Jerusalem Post.

Chapter 14
Securitization: Response to the Asian Challenge?

Introduction: *Historical Overview of Transatlantic Financial Relations*

Undoubtedly, modern finance helped shape post-Depression-post-War efforts at reconstruction. After the wars, states managed to convince skeptical spenders to trust it with their savings to be used for an important social call and that recycling such money into various infrastructural and social activities could have better social payoffs. Enter the bond market. It is capable of pulling two parties – the state and traditional big businesses on one hand and lenders on the other. The state joined in at another front in a big way.

It rallied against capital flights, which means it had to develop its own fundraising capacity. The Bretton Woods agreement became the defining document of this culture. For the U.S. state though, its geopolitical imperatives clouded this Bretton Woods spirit for obvious economic and political reasons. The Eastern Block and the Middle East, flush with petro-dollar cash, in the late 1970s, found a safe haven in the well-established financial Mecca of London. Recall it was a bit later, in 1979, that the Iranian/U.S. hostage crisis emerged. Eurocurrency was born, again, for political and economic reasons, to recycle the greenback so that political adversaries (including Iran) could lay hands on the greenback outside of the U.S. Indirectly, it had the effects of shoring up fixed exchange regimes. Countries under this regime needed it order to prop up their bond market capacities, key to national development efforts.

U.K.'s role here is intriguing given its unique past with the U.S. over the loss of its trading 'Kingdom' after the Lend Lease agreement. In this agreement, the U.S., then the official powerhouse of the world, traded the loss of U.K.s trading block for material and financial support for the latter's war efforts, all in the name of 'free trade'. The Marshall Plan (1947-50) and other Keynesian-friendly schemes became added sweeteners in the rebuilding of Europe. So whether inward-looking capacity-building exercises or under free trade, the U.K has always threaded the limits of competition and cooperation with the U.S.

At the back of U.K.'s mind, though, were skirmishes with the Dutch in the 17th century in Manhattan, and later disgust over President Richard Nixon's unilateral decision to end Bretton Wood's 'be each other's neighbor's' mission on that fateful Sunday, August 15, 1971. Put together, U.K.'s baggage centered on:

- ambivalence of how 'backed' exchanges should be
- mechanism to oversee it
- who should oversee it.

All these would eventually be tampered by securitization. Securitization cuts through them. Whether inward- or outward-looking, it makes national/regional projects happen with unlimited phantom money-creating capacity. More importantly, and substantively from corporate point of view, it is economical, much as it is politically and relatively culturally neutral. Central bank got creative here too in order to be relevant, building on its traditional mass-production and distribution infrastructure (phantom money-creation machine). To sum up, with handsome commission and fees to be made, London and New York have been all too wiling to co-host the world of exotics. Other countries fought for this privilege but in finance, traditions reign, so New York and the London – the transatlantic corridor - won out.

Shadow Banks and Securitization here to stay?

Without shadow banks, there would be no securitization within the present legal framework governing collateralized arrangements.

Securitization

Securitization, like all kinds of phantom moneys, frees up money for someone else to spend. Take the example of your spiffy $70,000 Land Rover made in U.K. Suppose, as was the case with VW beetle decades ago, that the automaker in U.K. decides not to make Land Rover vehicles again. Those already in possession of the car have a collector item – rare vehicles. You can create a contract on the worth of the car now to be sold to raise, say, $50,000 from willing 'investors'. That means the purchaser of this $50,000 bond has a $50,000 stake in your car. So long as the car value holds up all parties are happy – lender and car owner who borrowed. But if it turns out that Land Rover changes its mind and decides to resume production. Your car, quite old now, will be worth almost nothing, lucky to get $8,000 for it. Thus, both the buyer of the bond (lender) and you the seller lose, paper loss that could have serious aggregate/macroeconomic implications if a lot more people took the same position (raising money on a car they thought was rare but turned out to be the a lemon). Potential investors (those at the bottom of the pyramid) will flee. Unable to support the top of the pyramid, the system crashes. This is a mirror image of the present credit meltdown.

Under the gold standard, for instance, a dollar in currency had to be backed up by a collateral of a dollar. Latter on, *fractional reserve banking* reduced such one-to-one collateral to a mere fraction of 10% or less. This is the phantom money formula that this generation has come to know of, the last step toward total elimination of even the meager 10% Canada has since abolished as 'required reserve' of all deposited money at the commercial banks. Now it is free-for-all. Securitization essentially makes 'required reserve' redundant, permitting unlimited credit to be created.

The Magic of Fractional Reserve Banking

Freeing reserves creates even more phantom money by making more money available to lend. Such money in turn facilitates trade, boost demand for goods and services that otherwise would go unsold. After all, it is easier to spend borrowed money than shop with hard-earned savings. This is why this first aggressive attempt at 'liquefying' gold tucked away as 'savings' in bank's reserves made such a buzz then. Tucked away, it simply denied us of the pleasure of spending. Not so now. We get to spend them and even more. This is the magic of the multiplier.

A 10% collateral (required reserve) gives a multiplier value of $1/10\% = 10$ meaning every dollar deposited creates $10 in total loans. In other words, this one-to-ten multiple expansion of deposits turns a $100 deposit to $100 ($10) in collateral/required reserve, leaving $90($100-$10) to be lent out, 10 times in total (9 times in net loans plus 1 in collateral).

By way of timeline, even with our deposit-creating prowess back in the 1990s, we still saw it prudent to differentiate M_1, from M_2. The latter has savings accounts tagged on to cash and chequing account. M_3 was slightly differentiated from M_2 in the sense that a less liquid GIC (investment certificate) was added to M_2 and so on. In fact, such Ms could go on to as high as one wants to go, to, say, M_{200}, increasing in the degree of their illiquidity to include mortgage contracts. Now, securitization, a phenomenon that caught fire in the late 1970s, blurs the difference between M_1 and M_{200}.

Regulated banks whose culture revolved around the old Ms now have tolerated, adopted strategies, and coexisted with shadow banks, and so are now able to create unlimited amount of phantom money from any illiquid assets - from student loan contracts to mortgages down to credit card contracts. In other words differences between the Ms have disappeared because a debit card collapses all kinds of Ms to be used to buy houses, cars, clothes, furniture. Figure 1 points to this trend in such burgeoning household debt.

Ponzi applies a Centrifugal Force

Companies were the only agents that generally 'saved' money in the 1990s and in the new millennium. They should be because they were selling to the other side that was so busy buying with borrowed money created from thin air. But they also joined in the spending spree using these profits to either pay dividends to their owners (shareholders) or buy up other companies. Companies that pursue both strategies are looked on as good companies in the finance community. That

Figure 14.1: Household Financial Obligations as a Percent of Disposable
Personal Income (FODSP)

is why especially in good times, both lenders and borrowers get to overspend,
and since marginal (new) entrants to such bubble schemes are the ones to be hit
the hardest by financial collapse. The top of the 'pyramid' becomes too heavy for
such people at the bottom to support. Eventually it collapses. That is what the
world financial system is facing today, a Ponzi world that has Treasury/Finance
Department and central banks on standby to underwrite finance requests.

Section 6
The Exotics

Chapter 15
From Fixed Income to the Exotics

Introduction

Fearful lenders (buyers) want protection. Sellers of such contracts (insurance agents of sorts specializing in such products) need commission. Intermediaries wanting to make fast bucks from contract writing, including that of credit, all come to play here to make the (credit) derivative market happen. For the rest of this chapter, discussions will be on elements of this vast market, part of the sociology of debt culture.

Recall, in the introductory chapter, a $1.048 quadrillion number was thrown as bets on global GDP of $80 trillion. Again, using Bank of International Settlement data, of the number of contracts (notional amount) outstanding, interest rate derivatives took a hefty $350 trillion gross market value. The sheer size is an indication of fears in the direction of interest rate given the size of overspending. I get to the mechanics of bets by way of inverse floaters in a minute but it is important to mention that the most striking development in this derivative market is the evolution of credit default swap: invisible on the chart but $8 trillion worth by the time of the 2008 meltdown. Taking insurance on transactions for fear of default is an indication of suspicion of the health of borrowers/lenders. It has also important to drill home the point that of all these categories of derivatives, that on commodities was the most stable, indicating that the real side has always been a good bet.

Collateralized debt obligations (CDOs)

The latest incarnation in the bond craze is an entry-level class of 'mutual fund of exotic bonds' commonly referred to as collateralized debt obligations (CDOs), a bunch of different IOUs with different characteristics bundled together, some with risks easier to tell but others difficult. The mechanics is a bit involved so I stick with some stand-alone ones. The message here is that much as they could be used as defensive (insurance) tools, many a time users get carried away.

Inverse floaters

The same can be said of a class of modified straight bonds called inverse floaters. As demonstrated in the table 1 above, returns here on this fixed income security could be tweaked and considerably amplified, for better or for worse.

Credit Derivatives

As with inverse floaters, this class of insurance, a very popular one, has gained notoriety recently. At $30 trillion worth by Bank of International Settlement count by the second half of 2008, it has been blamed for serving as an assault weapon. What makes them so popular? I argue that it is because credit agencies do such a poor job at rating borrowers that the best way for a lender to protect self is to take insurance on such borrowers so that they could be paid when borrowers default.

Reasons for Popularity of Credit Derivatives

Filling the (in)efficiency Gap: Credit Derivatives to the rescue of credit bureaus

At the end of the day, there are triggers (underlying assets) like interest rates, stock prices, or currency values that make payouts happen. Lenders, unable or unwilling to check borrowers books for soundness, take such insurance so that loss due to default and uncertainties from these triggers (price of these underlying assets) could be cushioned.

Lenders take such precautions in large part because of complicated financial arrangements that they themselves sometimes do not understand fully. Even when they do, they tend to be rooted in uncertainty and buried in complicated and overlapping contracts. However, others emanates from mediocre performance of rating agencies that leave large holes for such contracts to emerge. A few of the complexities are:

- Hedge funds and their secretive ways of doing business make default assessment difficult, complicating efforts at verifying credit adequately.
- Financial statements are increasingly too complicated to accurately forecast risk inherent in firms
- So credit derivatives, somehow, picks up such residual risk that credit agencies leave behind. For a rational agent, therefore, this contract becomes an essential expense for protecting the downside, and even some upsides as well. In short, it buys peace of mind.

What exactly are Credit Derivatives anyway?

As financial assets, credit derivatives take their values from 'risky' bond market by trying to:

- isolate credit risk (risk of non-payment) from
- duration risk (risk for keeping bond for so long) and
- interest rate risk (interest rate inducing price of bond to change).

Secondly, they give investors the ability to buy all kinds of risks that they desire, or to isolate them from interest-rate risk. In this way, they could split the bond market for it to appeal to different groups, what some argue is an advantage. For example banks and insurance agencies might want to hold high-graded AAA bonds while hedge funds might want to go for riskier ones. This is where collateralized debt obligations (CDOs) comes in. Like mutual funds, it could fit many of such risk groups.

Uses of Credit Derivatives

It makes sense for lenders such as banks, and for insurance companies, pension and mutual funds to buy such contracts because

- the 'cost'/premium of this contract could very well be much less than the benefits of retrieving the loan
- For holders of bonds, they can keep for tax purposes and not give it up. Instead, they just buy protection for any default etc.
- Could be hidden (off-balance sheet) but with potential risk/benefits out of sight.

Proliferation of Credit Derivatives means Bad News for the Bond Market

As with every business transaction between two parties, one person's gain is the other one's loss, at least in the very short run. But over a period of time, even the most private of some of our interaction impacts (positively or negatively) on a 'third party' (externality, we call it), an effect that could be devastating if institutional response to them falls short as it did in 2008. Here is how.

Given past and recent default rates, private credit contracts between financial institutions (1st party) and others (2nd parties) have generated problems that the third party (taxpayers) ended up being seriously disadvantaged. The Savings and Loans (S&L) crisis left exactly such aftertaste, so did the present pension (Defined Benefit) crisis.

Credit derivatives, essentially arbiters of sorts, are relatively new and less standardized, unlike interest rate and equity derivatives. That is why participants use all kinds of lengthy documentation on terms of deals.

The pure insurance dimension to credit derivatives

These very insurance (derivatives) contracts could inadvertently create their own risks. That is, if more people get insurance for, say, protection against flooding, what happens in times of heavy rainfall that end up creating massive flooding? We get huge payouts from insurance companies. But huge loses could trigger even more instability by way of default (by insurance companies), creating even more chaos in the financial system. So one can see why too much insurance/ derivatives could be even more hazardous to our health.

Forms of Credit, risks, and credit derivatives design

Credit derivatives take the form of:

1. bonds, the most popular and standardized, and
2. loans.

Loans are more difficult to deal with because they vary in forms, shapes, and terms. Loans and bonds here are the reference assets - contract between the borrowers and the lenders on nature of compensation in times of adverse event on payback of loans and bonds. In general, derivatives are just pieces of paper/contracts/insurance, worthless in themselves but so long as we keep making deals (such as making loans and issuing bonds), then such contracts get to derive a lifeline, hence their name 'derivatives', instruments that spreads and/or transfer risks/return from one person to the (un)fortunate other(s). No wonder they are designed with an eye on foreign currencies (currency derivatives), commodity markets (commodity derivatives, equity/shares (equity derivatives), and credit markets (credit derivatives).

Specific Types of Credit Derivatives

1. SWAPS

Default Swap: the most popular of the three, are for nervous buyer seeking protection. You pay 'premium' in return for a payment in case of default, bankruptcy, insolvency etc.(total economic performance (interest and capital value change).

Total-rate-of-returns swap (TRORS): 'total return seller' pays a premium to protect self. Payouts involve total economic performance (interest and capital value change). A rise in price of an asset gives the buyer (banks etc) capital appreciation and in case of price decline pays depreciation value. A credit event terminates contracts, evoking settlement immediately.

2. OPTION

This is slightly different from the swaps in the sense that:

a. as with any other options contract, a buyer pays a 'premium' to a seller of the option who pockets the premium.
b. One does not have to wait for something/event to happen as in the case of default swap, only if there is a difference in the value of the bond. In other words, payoff is based on difference between the bond (reference asset) and interest rate swap with same maturity.

Inverse floater : The lethal Weapon of choice

Created from traditional bond issuers - collateralized mortgage obligation (CMO), municipal, and corporate issues - an inverse floater is a bond or other type of debt whose coupon rate has an inverse relationship to short-term interest rates. As interest rates rise, the coupon rate falls. As a consequence, with each coupon payment, the floating rate resets for the next period following:

floating rate = fixed rate – coupon leverage reference rate.

In other words, when short-term interest rates declines, an inverse floater holder benefits in two ways:

3. The bond appreciates in price
4. The yield increases

In the easiest form, a borrowing company/government buys the bond at par, gets into a swap agreement to get a fixed rate in exchange for LIBOR (British/ European equivalent of discount rate).

Mimicking Returns=x – LIBOR

we get:

$$\text{Returns} = \text{Fixed Rate} + \text{swap}$$
$$= 2(\text{Fixed rate}) - \text{Libor}$$

Stated differently, the present value gets us

$$PV = PV \, (2 \text{ Fixed rate}) - PV \, (LIBOR).$$

After approximations and
letting D as change and $\Delta PV(LIBOR) = 0$

$$\text{we get } \Delta PV = 2\Delta PV(\text{fixed})$$

So price sensitivity of this floater generates two times the reward that fixed rate bond generates, keeping LIBOR (short-term rate) influence minimal while long-term rate becomes important. This is what investors have to keep in mind.: twice the loss if interest rate goes the wrong way.

Section 7
Institutions that Mainstreamed the Debt Culture

Chapter 16
Money-Creating Machines Fulfilling the Growth and Low Inflation Promise

Introduction: A Culture Sketched

Growth has been the key economic policy objective in virtually all countries. In such polities, two key institutions are entrusted, officially, with the mantle to cheerlead such a push. They even have the constitutional muscles to pull all the gadgets out of their cultural toolbox to do just that. In the United States, for instance, the Civil-War-Era National Bank Act bestowed such power of issuing national bank notes to federal chartered banks (Kregel, 2010:2) but then rewarded states with clients who would manage their own checkable deposits, under the supervision of The Fed, the very agency that oversees bank notes issues. This is the extent to which the ideological left and right agree: on supervision. Of what kind and the capability at promoting progressive outcomes is a different story. Specifically, it is about access to credit and the 'non-neutrality' issue.

That is, the issue with the left is not whether 'money matters'. Afterall, this proposition has been validated throughout this book. Rather, it is the fear that credit and money, not quite the neutral 'medium of exchange' that we find in mainstream textbooks, has significant distributional consequences as well, much as they are instruments for sectoral distortions.

Tabloid narration of this leftist stance spells out activism in the form of jobs for 'Main Street'. The ideological right, on the otherhand, tend to pin their hopes on price/interest rate stability. Seeking to preserve financial asset values (on Wall Street), the right leaves itself wide open to the leftist distributional charge. But the past decade and a half before the 2008 meltdown quickly erased this chasm. Both sides won their respective fights without firing a shot. In fact so good was the growth outcome that even though the core value differences still exist among them, the two sides did converge. Here is how.

- Emerging economies were able to export deflation to the rest of the world via exports, ushering in a low-low prices and low-low interest rate climate. The ideological right was happy, in fact so excited that it seemed to forget the old menace (debt). In fact so fearless that the Ricardian

Equivalent strand of the right saw it as desirable so long as such IOUs are not owned by foreigners. In short, inflation has not been a problem so both the left and the right have not had such negative distributive issues in their respective constituencies to quibble about.

- Both financial and real sectors rode on the cocktail of these lead financial sector activities. Expectedly, growth in output and in employment followed. Full-employment ideals were all met here too, with even increased productivity to boot. Indeed, these were golden years for the larger (Main Street) society as well as Wall Street that run through it. There were plenty of jobs, with lots of leftover income to recycle in the bond market.

- Governments were also in the gay mood, expectedly, as taxes rolled in from all sides.

- As for The Fed and other central banks worldwide, their constitutional role as liquidity providers made it all too important. However, the new order has them accommodating key players in the financial market. It did not matter the magnitude of bonds to be unloaded to meet such objectives. Even for the left, so long as this drift in culture managed to bring home the bacon, it was willing to support it.

Thus, under the aforementioned climate of expected low-inflation, all classes of interest rates kept falling, making investment as we know it all too predictable. That was why 'bookies' did not even take bets on such financial papers. Recall, 'investment' in financial assets is about the forecasting the direction of interest rates. If outcome (low expected interest rate) is predictable in downward direction, 'bookies' lose.

Back in Las Vegas before the February 11, 1990, Buster Douglas-Mike Tyson fight, bookies were not taking bets on Mike Tyson winning because he was so dominant that he was expected to win. Rather, they took bets on what round (derivative) Douglas would be dropped. Interest rates too were supposed to go down, not up, meaning the so-called yield curve was reversed (inverted). Thus, betters needing high returns had to go exotic. This is how gambling made its way into contracts and into our psyche, an issue discussed in chapter 11. So rather than support a higher-savings culture, The Fed and other central banks around the world tacitly supported a high-consumption one by accommodating the avalanche of savings pouring in from high-saving countries in exchange for IOUs.

The Money Agencies

We know Treasury Department (Finance Ministry) is the dominant political arm of the government entrusted with the responsibility of seeing to it that the growth promise is fulfilled and that governmental machinery runs smoothly to support it. To be specific, this spending and revenue agency, in addition to setting the budgetary framework, it is relied on to see through reconstruction especially after wars, as we found out in immediate post-War reconstruction time. That is why anytime the government spends more than it takes in the form of taxes, it (Treasury Dept) has to figure out ways of pay for it, the reason why in almost every country, Finance Ministries oversee Internal Revenue Services. To rehash these points, Finance Ministries

1.   borrow money through the bond market from anyone - citizen or foreigners - with pocket change to spare by issuing IOUs called Treasury Bills, named after itself (treasury), $10.6 trillion of it for the U.S. before the 2008 credit meltdown, and a bit of Treasury-bonds, and national savings bonds as well.

2.   It can also order, as the bureaucratic heavyweight, The Fed or any Ministry of Finance, to *print money*, a point I get into next.

The art of Printing Money: 3 examples to draw from

The Printing of money: no taxpayer required

Literally, printing money means the central bank pawns its own IOUs by paying for it. That is, it takes second or even third mortgages on them. Put differently, it buys its own IOUs (called treasury bills/bonds) issued on earlier borrowing, and other corporate IOUs floating around. By buying its own IOU debt, it borrows twice, three times etc. It can afford to in the sense that it can print money to buy them. In the last four months of 2008 alone, for instance, The Fed in the United States added over $2 trillion to the red column of its balance sheet by exchanging/printing money in return for questionable assets from failing banks so that the chartered banks could lend them out, a process commonly referred to as *recapitalization*. So long as the political boss, the Treasury Department, goes along with such plans, and usually it does, it could make things happen. Those bad assets are then instantly switched into reserves from which these banks can draw from for use as they see fit, usually to lend to clients.

Recent examples

Fed to Buy $1 Trillion in Securities to Aid Economy was Andrews (2009)[1] lead article in the NY Times. This $1 trillion was in addition to the nearly $1.2 trillion that had been pumped into the economy since the last quarter of 2008, all through the purchase of existing government IOUs from banks and non-bank public. But with all the hoopla, the central banks can only go that far – by pumping money into the banks hoping someone would do the borrowing, and borrow we have. That did

•   rev up the mortgage market
•   put $750 billion into buying useless government-guaranteed mortgage-backed securities in addition to the $500 billion is in the works.
•   Another $300 billion went into longer-term Treasury securities with the intent to increase price and force interest rates down. Yield on 30-year Treasury bond fell precipitously to 3.4% from 3.75% immediately after the announcement. Stock market rose but the dollar fell by about 3 percent

against key currencies, a sign that the two audiences – international and domestic – are speaking different languages.

Bailouts, the new name for printing of notes

1.   The GMAC saga

So The Fed is able to create money and also create institutions around it, literally. It also has the ability to pull the plugs from underneath them as well. The former was exercised in the guise of capitalizing GMAC in the last quarter of 2008, part of a tsunami of financial shakeup in the United States and in Europe in the last half of 2008. Even bigger was its addition of Merrill Lynch (founded 1914) to Bank of America's collection on September 15, 2008 even as it let Lehman Brothers (founded 1850) die on the same day. As for Bear Stearns (founded 1923), JPMorgan swallowed it up, then took on GMAC too.

2.   Now, call it GMAC Bank

Goldman Sachs, founded in 1869, was next, transformed into a bank holding company on September 21, 2008, so was Morgan Stanley, founded in 1935, again, both decisions made on the same day, all engineered ostensibly to help the real side by making money available to lend. Then came General Motors turn in December 2008.

Within this mandate as a creator of commercial banks, The Fed, rather than nationalize it (swap money for toxic assets) made a private bank out of GMs financial arm (GMAC) so as to entitle it to a piece of The Fed's bailout money. That meant Cerberus Capital Management, the private equity firm that had a 51 percent stake in GMAC, had to give up part of its control in order to let The Fed (government) in. Chrysler Finance was not that lucky. It was left alone as the finance arm of Chrysler.

3.   The IndyMac sale, and the undoing of its Bank Status

With a large sub-prime exposure, in July 2008, The Fed called IndyMac Bancorp insolvent, the second biggest bank to fail in 2008. Thirty three of IndyMac's branches that had served as its reverse-mortgage units were subsequently put on the chopping block. That was not all. The $176 billion loan-servicing portfolio that it had was also sold to, among others in the consortium, private equity firms by name J.C. Flowers & Company and Dune Capital Management, and hedge fund company Paulson & Company. The Fed also pulled off similar feats by arranging the sale of troubled Wachovia and Washington Mutual (WaMu), other giant banks.

Standard Drawing Rights (SDR)

The final money-creating mechanism is Standard Drawing Right (SDR). This is the world's scheme to print money from United Nations offices - International Monetary Fund offices, to be exact, April 2009 its biggest day. The sum of $250 billion was allotted on this day at the G20 meeting in London. Like coupons, they were allocated as reserves on the basis votes, the table below illustrative of the proportions.

Table 16.1: Whose Vote Counts?

	Share %	
	Existing	Proposed
United States	16.77	16.73
Japan	6.02	6.23
Britain	4.86	4.29
France	4.86	4.29
China	3.66	3.81
Russia	2.69	2.39
Belgium	2.09	1.86
India	1.89	2.34
South Korea	1.38	1.36
Brazil	1.38	1.72

Source:IMF

Note

1. Andrews, A. **"Fed to Buy $1 Trillion in Securities to Aid Economy"** *NYT* **Mar 19.**

Chapter 17
Interest Rates: The True Universal Language

Introduction

Other than regulations, maintaining law and order, and the provision of services deemed essential (military, utilities etc), there is a forth front of (central) government responsibility that we take for granted. It is the maintenance of liquidity, monopoly reserved for the state. Had such monopoly not been granted, many of us would have machines in our homes to print all the paper money that we need.

Providing liquidity does not mean that governments goes around doling out cash to the citizenry, though it has done a bit of that lately. Liquidity just means those with a concept to sell (call it 'business plan') one can count on the two money departments – The Fed and Treasury Department – to spearhead organizational efforts at getting them the funds from, you guessed it, the bond market where people from all corners of the globe get to spare their pocket change. These two agencies work in concert, as discussed in chapter 16, have regulatory oversight over other financial institutions to provide liquidity. In return, lenders get their IOU receipt with a promised returns called interest (coupon) rate, usually calculated in a number of ways including the difference in the purchase price of the IOU and the amount that you get when you sell it at maturity. Other IOUs just state the return, say 5% of the principal.

And as with all goods/services, lots of bonds in the market imply somebody is borrowing too much so lenders demand higher 'price' for their loan, pushing interest rate up. The reverse is true when borrowing slows relative to savings. Here, those with money to spare have to shop harder for clients. The downside is that they have to scale back expectations of return/interest rate. The latter scenario is, for now, history. The former is real, evidenced by the avalanche of IOUs thrown at this bond market lately.

Earlier on in May 2009, weak demand for especially government bonds (due to excessive borrowing) - 30-yr US Treasury IOUs - forced the Treasury Department in the United States to retreat to re-price them (lower the price) so that it could yield higher interest rate/returns in order to make it attractive to lenders/buyers. In this particular British and U.S. cases, expectations of high future interest rate touched off a selling frenzy amidst fears that, at least fiscally, the worst was yet to come, and that the government might even find it harder to raise all these tens of trillions of dollars to finance its stimulus ideas and other fiscal priorities. Britain, especially, found this out the hard way too. On March 25, the offer of 40-yr IOUs, 1.75 billion pounds ($2.55 billion) attracted only 1.63 billion pounds ($2.37 billion).

Looking for More

For applicants for such 'easy money' (credit) before the crisis hit in 2008, the more exotic the plan presented to financial institutions, the better the chance for a bigger loan. For example a hedge fund with questionable worth seeking multi-billion dollar loan to acquire a target company stood a better chance of getting a loan than a s smaller company with a plain vanilla plan. Thus, banks, back then, were likely to give loans for grandiose project than plain vanilla ones just because they could bet on handsome returns without much thought on the downside. Afterall, at the time, there were many of such grandiose projects that managed to produce the desired returns and even more, and the two money departments were all too willing go along with such generous requisition.

Put together, as per monetary theory, these two money departments 'determine' bond market, and bond market determines interest rates, and interest rates determine the price of bonds, and bond price help determine policy. These interactions have come to be known as:

1. *money* or monetary policy (interest rate policy) and
2. *credit* policy,

all intended to influence economic activity, and boy, did the U.S. government deliver at both fronts. It did (a) by delivering low-low interest, reinforcing U.S. dominance in the bond (money market) as the largest borrower, and as an agent capable of spreading growth. But it has also proved that despite the growth potential, it can also export financial and economic crises throughout the world. Afterall, that is what happens when the price of anything drops so low. Basic economic theory suggests there will be excessive demand for them, and in this case there was more demand for credit from (risky) borrowers. Politicians also will always be around to brag for securing such low, low interest rate, supporting the culture that fosters it.

By politicizing this 'price' of money, interest groups (financial institutions, mortgage houses, some consumer groups, politicians, governments as borrowers) end up butting heads especially in times of crisis in an endless cycle of finger-pointing. Don't forget bankers. They square off with everyone else who dared label them greedy, and against, ironically, the very institutions (Freddie Mac and Fannie Mae) that promoted the culture of *access*. But a more lasting legacy needs special mention here.

These quasi-government agencies succeeded in taking securitization to a whole different level at a time when worldwide productivity and economic growth in itself could have provided the needed deflationary pressures for lower interest rates. But the money agencies, perhaps inadvertently, were on a mission to feed financial institutions and brokers with the commission needed to keep the debt culture going.

Governments and their preference. High or low interest rate?

So in this debt culture is the preference for high or low interest rate? To begin this discussion let us not forget stories of governments not ever paying their debt off. It is widely known that governments just creates inflation ever so slowly in order to eat into its debt. Granted there are now indexed bonds that smart lenders can buy to cover that part, the reality is that many lenders somehow look the other way.

Higher prices means a $100 debt will be worth increasingly less, say $97 this year, $95 next year, $93 a year after etc. Over time, these governments might succeed in wiping off most of its value. But higher inflation too implies higher interest rate because lenders, expecting depreciation of the worth of their loans will demand higher compensation – interest rate – for their trouble. Why then do I say that low-low interest rate has been the principal objective of the U.S. federal government knowing that higher inflation/interest rate has been good for its pocket book as it debt shrinks?

It is because low-low interest rate generates 'economies of scale'. That draws in a huge pool of people of all ethno-social stripes to be able to work, pay taxes, buy stuff, afford credit cards, buy cars, furniture, houses, appliances etc. Banks get their cut with generous commissions and fees to live large on. With this many people employed and borrowing to spend, government's social assistance bill declines significantly. The electorate, appreciative of this low-low inflation/unemployment environment, duly rewards politicians who tootle their horns for presiding over highest debt/home ownership rates. This keeps the culture going. Thus, even without the high inflation to eat away government debt, the pre-crisis low-interest culture was the preferable alternative.

The True Universal Language

True universal language, anyone? It is not English, not French, not Spanish, not Mandarin, and certainly not Hausa. It is not even money because there are still variants of money kicking around with all kinds of symbolism to share. It is interest rates, the true 'price' of money. Money as we know it is a key object of transfer, and interest rate acts as the dialect to interpret the value of money.

We have the prime rate, discount rate, and kinds of predatory rates all supposed to collapse forms of money into an index that everyone can understand. When this index is deemed too high, it is frowned on by different socio-economic groupings, generating passion on morality of policy and of policymakers. Ribaa, for instance, under Islamic Banking and usury, under some Christian faiths, draw ethical stares from which they manage to get the inspiration to proscribe such excesses. But by and large, interest rates of all kind becomes a universal measuring rod of worth.

Interest Rates. What rate?

Recall, a bond is priced, like all goods, at auction of sorts with 100 as a reference point. A price over 100, say 105, represents a premium, a sign of optimism. If under 100, say 93, we have a discount meaning expectations of problems ahead. If buyers settle on this (discount) price of 97, then the difference of 3 (100-97) will generate interest rate of this difference and related purchase price (97) yielding 3/97 = 3.07% in interest rate. A larger discount of, say, 92 indicates uncertainty, generating a higher interest rate of 6/92=6.5%.

Think about it. If you want to buy a car and you get a word that it is being recalled, you will want to buy this defective item at a discount. In other words, the high discount implies demand for high 'interest rate'. Generally, if lower interest rate is anticipated, future interest rate will be lower. This is reflected in the inverse *yield curve* that we hear so much of in finance stories and in textbooks. Conversely, if high future interest rate is expected, we have normal yield curve phenomenon at hand. The reference rate, as told, is the U.S. government (borrowing) one called T-bill rate, the premier dialect that the world models its languages (interest rates) around.

All in all, smaller, less 'secured' governments (they issue Munis) and bigger companies pay more than bigger (central) governments. Thus, these smaller entities issue straight bonds with higher interest rates than T-bills issued by central governments.

Interest rate. What kinda interest rate, or yield?

1. Coupon rate or simple interest rate: the promised rate divided by the face value. A $50 per annum coupon on a $1,000 face –valued bond yields$50/$1000 = 5%
2. current yield: is payoff you get if you do not buy the bond at face value. For the $1,000 bond, let us suppose you bought it for $900 with a coupon of $50, then the current yield will be $50/$900=5.56%
3. Yield-to-maturity: this most widely used measure takes into consideration your coupon's worth as well as that of the principal. Let us suppose your $1,000 bond gives you a $100 coupon this time. For a 3-yr bond the YTM will be PV= $100/(1+r) + 100/(1+r)2 + 100/(1+r)3 + 1000/(1+r)3 =$987.67 finding the r gives you the YTM: whether over the 3-yr period you gained/lost money. If a bond table not around you can use

r» FV – Purchase price
          # of yrs to maturity
(face value + purchase price)/2

The relationship between YTM and time gives us the Yield curve, how much your returns match up over time.

4. Discount yield: is the return on money market instrument such as T-bill. For instance if you bought a91-day govt. of Canada T-bill with a $1000 FV(expressed as a 100) for $972.76. Discount yield will be

$$\frac{100\text{-price}}{\text{price}} \times \frac{365}{\text{time}} =$$

$$\frac{100\text{-}97.276}{1.276} \times \frac{365}{91} = \frac{11.23\%}{}$$

5. Yield to call is different from YTM only in the sense that it takes into account the call date instead of the maturity date (please stay tuned for the next section on this).

Debentures are increasingly popular among this class of IOUs, secured just by good names. Foreign governments too get their own that they call Eurobonds, all carrying higher rates than T-Bills. Put together, the 'risky' corporate AA and the more riskier CC bonds carry correspondingly high interest rates (positive beta) than the more 'secure' Munis that in turn has a higher interest rate than T-Bills. In otherwords, they all pay a little more than T-bill rate by a fraction of beta (market risk), ostensibly to make up for the remote possibility of default.

Longer duration (5, 10, 15, 20 years etc) of bonds also suggests that anything can happen during the lifetime of such bonds so a bit higher returns is demanded by lenders. This gives the yield curve the upward sloping relationship interpreted as higher yield for bonds with longer maturity date (say 10 yrs) compared to say one maturing in 3 years.

Going for broke

There is something cute, even sexy, about gambling. The same cannot be said about patience. Patience is associated with the ageing and for those with money to spare too, lending to big governments (buying treasury bills IOUs) is boring. The guarantee of 'money back' is assumed but lenders want a lot more than just this alpha (α).

Technically, your savings (y) gets you α, what we call risk-free return - your reward for taking almost no risk on a T-bill. That makes you a conservative investor (second pie chart below). The first chart is an aggressive investor. That means, for the conservative investor, equation $y = \alpha + ß X$ nets a zero ß, turning it into $y = \alpha + 0 = \alpha$.

Figure 17.1: Agressive and Conservative Portfolios

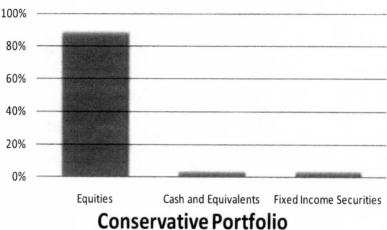

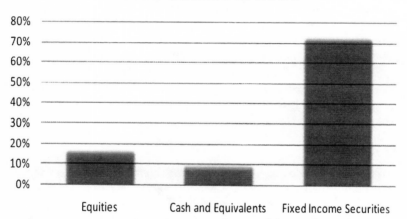

Not to be undone, at the supply side, issuers/borrowers (governments and companies) long associated with this 'old' class of savers sought the 'young' by adding layers of betas, introducing new layers of risks in the process. Conscious of this trend, those at the demand side (borrowers: government and bigger companies) are going exotic too, upping the ante with better return offers. With these otherwise safe T-bills, where from these returns? Issuers (borrowers) are sticking in insurance clauses that, like insurance sale, yields premiums to be split with lenders in a form of higher returns. This down side is usually conveniently ignored so long as good times roll on. That is what happened to the sub-prime (sub-creditworthy) borrowers. They ignored the downside, one element being the reset from the teaser (low-interest) to a higher interest rate/principal payment.

Section 8
Epilogue

Chapter 18
Epilogue: The Regulatory Misfire

Introduction

"Sex, drugs, and rock and roll" go together very well as a broad cultural doctrine. The same goes for the culture of debt sketched throughout this book. Even the most restrained spenders have a hard time resisting the lure of credit. For lenders, too, the incentive is there to oblige, given the generous fees that come from marginal borrowers who tend to be keenly aware that it is only through higher fees that they (marginal borrowers) get access to credit. The left's fear of non-neutrality is somewhat neutralized, albeit costly.

The securitization-related money that credit brings increases the money supply, helping to reduce interest rates for marginal borrowers and in the end, reducing the interest rate differential among all borrowers. If the objective is managing such liquidity, then the very incentives that nurture these institutions around securitization need to be reined in. But given the regulatory response so far, not questioning the status quo is the regimen, and the disease is being tackled just by dealing with the symptoms. Thus, I contend that *financial reform* bills floating around legislatures in the PIIGGS and in the United States only seem set to postpone the inevitable just a bit longer.

The Old (structural) Order Changeth, giving way to the New

Given that we are deeply immersed in the new culture of securitization, the thesis here is that we are just postponing the inevitable (crises). I say this because judging from the legislative initiatives that have either become law or about to become law, it is clear that countries around the world lack the resolve to confront the challenge ahead. That is, we know that even the modest Volcker Rule call for the crafting of regulations for investment banks or hedge funds keep their winnings and their losses while leaving chartered banks "public" to be bailed out when need be was not fully heeded judging by the provisions in the just passed Dodd-Frank Financial Wall Street and Consumer Protection Act, and Volcker Rule is very modest compared to the old values defined by Glass Steagall.

This regulatory drift is not surprising given that key thinkers like Kragel (2010)[1] added his voice to the chorus of those who wants no turning back to the old order. Perhaps the most telling is a story told in the editorials of the Economist[2] on Aug 3rd, 2010.

The story goes that what was left of the (September, 2007) nationalized Northern Rock is now the medium-sized bank called Northern Rock Plc. Essentially, this new handiwork was supposed to be a Glass-Steagall type – to be a traditional bank with a shiny mortgage book wiped clean with a low-low (0.7%) of loans in arrears for more than 3 months, substantially less than the national average of 2.37%. But with all this start, apparently, the first half of 2010 was not very kind to Northern Rock Plc. It could not make a profit. In fact it lost $210 million. Clearly, relying on interest spread on simple loans was not enough. In contrast, its spin-off [the old (private)] Northern Rock Asset Management was able to chalk up a handsome profit of $523 million for peddling its supposedly toxic assets. So clearly, engaging in those exotics clearly pays. So do not count on Glass-Steagall to come back. The old order surely has changed, given way to the new. So, any wind of change to turn the clock back? Yes, in part, I argue. Whether it will translate into constructive actions it a whole new story. I get to this next.

The Appetite for Change: Two Sides of the Thinking Aisle

The first side of dream architecture is a minimalist self-regulatory club (U.K., U.S., Ireland) that Gordon Brown actively led before his departure in the first quarter of 2010. We can loosely fit the PIIGGS in general in here too. They lived their neoliberal lives together, crashed together, and now talk reforms together, and will likely rise up together. In effect, they represent one side of the debate, on how best to soft-land. The other side, also within the Euro region, has more activist fire in them. Expectedly, they are countries that reached into activism as a key (macroeconomic) cultural defense — France and Germany, for example. There is a real-side detour of relevance here.

Schwartz (2009)[3] gave an account of stimulus projects' effectiveness in such activist countries relative to the United States in particular. Contrasted with France, a country in the activist group, Schwartz argued, 75% of the $37 billion stimulus plan had been spent by mid-2009 in France, targeted to projects that year. The aim, to the French, was to maintain their cultural patrimony and keep key structures and monuments in pristine condition — to fix chateaus, cathedrals, and museums. In the United States, similar "Keynesian" projects targeted to fixing potholes and building and fixing bridges did not quite take off until recently. The difference in vision between these two worlds? It is the disparity in state capacity and efficiency. Unfortunately, approaches to the financial market also reflect this ghost of a structural difference at the real side. Going by this trend in reforms in the trans-Atlantic hub, you may expect a sequel to this book in ten years — the life cycle to financial crises — and perhaps it will take the life cycle of another crisis to flush out such excesses.

This activist group gets support from a likely source, a looser coalition of Asian giants with vibrant real sides, and a number of non-traditional economists, especially those of the left. Together, they advocate a more comprehensive regulation of the regulator as well as the regulated, while the former points only to the regulator. In other words, the struggle is about how much control the regulator needs over the regulated, and whether the two key institutions — central banks and the Financial Services Authority — should wield as much power as they do now. There is also tension between the cultural and legal differences on both sides of the Atlantic: the European side that has long had one-stop shopping for banking, where every contract (including derivatives) could be bought, for a fee of course; and between interventionists and freewheeling free-marketers at both sides.

The Final Bill

The PIIGGS' proposal that emerged in the U.S. Congress was obviously a photocopy of an earlier, pacesetting white paper unveiled by British Finance Minister Alistair Darling on June 7, 2009. It appeared exactly a year after that, in June 2010.

What It Did Not Do

Ashkenas (2010)[4] set the tone for this section with a concern as to "Why the Latest Financial Reform Bills Won't Prevent Another Crisis." He urged policymakers to go beyond the re-labeling of the job descriptions of regulators. Another concern to him was how even with the narrow focus on the regulators, the present policy drift was not able to reduce complexity, overlaps in jurisdictions, and fragmentation within the roster of standard-setting agencies — the Financial Accounting Standards Board, NYSE, and the ratings agencies, all of which vie for turf control. In summary:

1.   For starters, under this bill, Fannie Mae and Freddie Mac, the two quasi-government agencies that mainstreamed securitization and cheap loans, and made houses affordable, are still in business, effectively taken over by the government.
2.   Obviously, they will live to see another day, and that "public" and "private" investment and banking are still joined to the hip. Thus, public banks can still be free with your money (rather than with their own "shareholders' equity").
3.   Derivatives practices also stay as they are. The hope had been that banks, as "public institutions" (as was the case under Glass–Steagall) would be forced to spin off a good chunk of the estimated $600-plus OTC derivatives being redirected to exchange (centralized) houses called "separately capitalized subsidiaries," a move that would have been somewhat in line with the Volcker Rule — but the banks managed to fight off the pressure and claimed exemptions for commodities and

energy swaps, implying that they get to stay in the derivatives business.
4.   Moreover, since a chunk of the meltdown was related to mortgage
      contracts that consumers did not understand but were duped to sign
      up for anyway, the hope was that at the minimum, applications would
      be streamlined the way they are in Canada. Legal clinics to help such
      gullible and unsuspecting applicants spread out among the 50 states, all
      with different applications and layers of brokers to match. This leaves
      the crookery aspect of mortgages intact.

What It Does

What it does is dump two of the nine key agencies with regulatory powers
over the financial markets, and then sets up the so-called FSA (Financial Services
Authority). It introduces one more agency, the National Bank Supervisor, which
in effect is part of a Consumer Financial Protection Agency with oversight
authority over issues that were previously spread out over seven agencies. So
the Darling Plan, as with the Gartner one, designates the Council for Financial
Stability to track hiccups along the way, and still roots the financial lifeline in the
same self-regulatory tripartite machine: Treasury, the Bank of England (The Fed
in the United States), and the Financial Services Authority (FSA).

The latter will be the consumer advocate, which will keep consumers informed
on risk and management effectiveness. That is, they will just be required to give
annual progress reports on risk-taking and bonuses, and take up new powers to
impose penalties against misconduct. As Fernholz (2008:1) wrote:

"The shocking part of this plan was the new powers it gave to The Fed to
identify systematic risk. It is supposed to do this by first identifying the size/
leverage. If it is too big to fail, then more capital/leverage requirements would
be needed. But this is an agency that has had a hard time identifying such risk
themselves."[5]

So, once again, with so many blanks left unfilled, expect a sequel to this
book, once the ten-year cycle comes around.

Notes

1. Kragel, Jan (2010) *Is This a Minsky Moment for Reform of Financial Regulation?* Levy Institute Working Paper # 586, 2010
2. The Economist (2010) *So You Wanted a Narrow Bank*, Aug 3
3. Bernard Schwartz, "Stimulus Effectiveness." *New York Times,* 6 July 2009
4. Ron Ashkenas, "Why the Latest Financial Reforms Won't Prevent Another Crisis." *Harvard Business Review,* 29 June 2010.
5. Tim Fernholz, "Who Regulates the Regulators?" *The American Prospect,* 19 June 2008.

Index